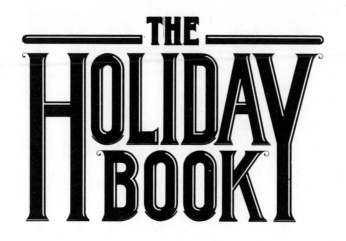

THE HOLIDAY BOOK

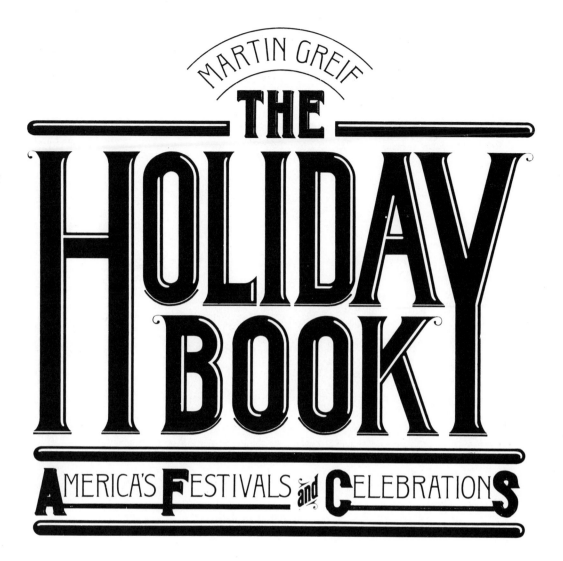

MARTIN GREIF

THE HOLIDAY BOOK

AMERICA'S FESTIVALS and CELEBRATIONS

The Main Street Press

A Main Street Press Book

Universe Books
New York

For Phyllis Edwards and Marion McCormack

First Edition, 1978

All Rights Reserved

Copyright © 1978 by The Main Street Press

Library of Congress Catalog Card Number 77–91924

ISBN 0–87663–980–5 paperback edition
309–2 cloth edition

Published by Universe Books
381 Park Avenue South
New York City 10016

Produced by The Main Street Press
42 Main Street
Clinton, New Jersey 08809

Every possible effort has been made to locate
sources and copyright owners. If oversights have occurred,
they will be corrected in subsequent printings.

Contents

To most Americans, including many of those who most ardently consider themselves true-blue sons and daughters of the Stars and Stripes, a holiday is little more than a day off from work. Washington's Birthday, Memorial Day, Labor Day, Columbus Day, and Thanksgiving have become—irrespective of their original meanings—excuses for long weekends, enjoyed at home in front of the television set or, just as likely, on the road dodging trucks and campers and avoiding the possibility of becoming a statistic on the mounting list of traffic fatalities. Other holidays—Valentine's Day, St. Patrick's Day, Mother's Day, Father's Day, Halloween—are superficially observed, largely because our memories are prodded by the appearance of greeting cards in store windows a month or more before the events themselves. (If not for these commercial displays, in fact, far too many of us in the final quarter of the twentieth century would be practically unaware of the holidays that mark the changing seasons of the year.) Still other holidays—Lincoln's Birthday, Arbor Day, May Day, Flag Day, and Veterans Day among them—if observed in any way at all, become the subjects of thirty-second "human interest" spots on the 7 o'clock news or mere items buried on page fifty-six of the evening newspaper.

Yet there is nothing new in any of these mild complaints. More than eighty years ago, in the lengthening shadow of the superpatriotic Centennial celebration of 1876, President Grover Cleveland registered a similar complaint: "The American people are but little given to the observance of public holidays," he said. "The commemoration of the day on which American independence was born has been allowed to lose much of its significance as a reminder of providential favor and of the inflexible patriotism of the fathers of the republic, and has nearly degenerated into a revel of senseless noise and aimless explosion, leaving in its train far more of mishap and accident than lessons of good citizenship or pride of country. The observance of Thanksgiving Day is kept alive through its annual designation by Federal and State authority. But it is worth our while to inquire whether its original meaning, as a day of united praise and gratitude to God for the blessings bestowed upon us as a people and as individuals, is not smothered in feasting and social indulgence. We, in common with Western nations everywhere, celebrate Christmas, but how much less as a day commemorating the birth of the Redeemer of mankind than as a day of hilarity and the interchange of gifts."

Grover Cleveland's intentions in speaking out on "Patriotism and Holiday Observance" were honorable and sincere. But, as we can readily see, nothing has changed from his day to ours except the accelerated degree of informality and leisure that mark our public days. It is, of course, just as futile to expect Americans to observe all holidays with high seriousness as it is to attempt to turn back the clock to a time when most did. We should be grateful, in fact, that American democracy itself encourages free people to be "but little given to the observance of public holidays." Here, after all, there is no armed guard to herd people into the streets to enact a forced salute to the national flag. The right *not* to observe a public day, as we should remember, is one of the blessings of democracy.

The purpose of this book, then, is not to point an accusing finger at the many who have forgotten (if, in fact, they ever knew) the meanings of our holidays and festivals. Rather, it is meant to inform (and to delight) those whose curiosity about our "days and deeds" goes beyond the packaged sentiment or puerile humor of a modern greeting card. A celebration of American celebrations in pictures, words, and poetic song, *The Holiday Book* is intended as a source book for teachers, students, parents, and all those who want to inquire into the rich lore of our traditions as exemplified in our festival days.

The Holiday Book deals with the notable holidays and festivals observed in America and, through informational essays, primary source material, and documentary illustrations, explores how and why these holidays came into being, their history, and their customs and observance—both past and present. The book includes full chapters on twenty holidays and summary information on twenty more. Although all nationally-observed holidays are discussed, as well as many of local interest (such as Cinco de Mayo, Patriots' Day, or Jefferson Davis's Birthday), *The Holiday Book* does not pretend to completeness. Omitted, for example, are most religious holidays with the exception of Easter and Christmas, two Christian festivals that have a special place in American cultural history and have passed through the central melting pot of the New World to emerge in unique American forms—a cultural phenomenon that has not affected, say, the observance of Good Friday or of Rosh Hashana, the Jewish New Year. Omitted, too, are such special days as National Cheese Day or Aviation Day that, although of undoubted importance to their respective observers, have not generally caught the public imagination. Admittedly, the individual reader can debate the virtues of including Arbor Day and May Day as "major" holidays since both have fallen into the limbo of indifference in recent years. Yet both days played special roles in American history and, in our highly mechanized era, should be profitably revived as reminders of America's roots in the unspoiled earth. Think of it: holidays, sad to say, are among our only remaining cultural links to the changing of the seasons.

The United States Congress has declared nine federal legal public holidays: New Year's Day, Washington's Birthday, Memorial Day, Independence Day, Labor Day, Columbus Day, Veterans Day, Thanksgiving Day, and Christmas Day. Much to the consternation of many traditionalists, five of these days have been observed on Mondays since January 1, 1971: Washington's Birthday (third Monday in February), Memorial Day (last Monday in May), Labor Day (first Monday in September), Columbus Day (second Monday in October), and Veterans Day (fourth Monday in October).* Although the individual states set the legal dates for holidays (federal holidays are official only in Washington, D.C., and in federal agencies), custom dictates that these nine major American holidays are to be observed on the same day throughout the nation.

In addition to providing essential information about the primary holidays of the American year, *The Holiday Book* is in part a nostalgic recreation of the national past. By invoking the literature and graphic arts of a distant day—primarily the nineteenth century, but no later than the period of the First World War—we can come not only closer to the sources of our customs and observances, but to an understanding as well of a time when patriotism was a virtue, simple and unashamed in its unabashed down-home innocence and sincerity. Much of the poetry in particular is charged with an emotional intensity that suggests the uniqueness of American democracy in the troubled world of the nineteenth century. Much of it, by modern standards, is

*Traditionalists have won at least one battle. A new federal law dictates that as of 1978 Veterans Days will once again be observed on November 11.

not poetry at all, but, rather, light verse or even doggerel. But these verses—pulsating with the patriotism of the early Republic—provide an index of American sentiment and feeling about national events that are only dimly remembered and observed today. As such, they are documents at least as valuable in the history they reflect as the finer artifacts of the past, holding as they do a mirror to the social and cultural heritage of America. The illustrations—woodcuts, lithographs, engravings, and posters—require no apology or explanation. For a nation that had turned consciously away from the religious and regal images of the Old World, these graphics provided a visual vocabulary of secular icons—eagles, banners, and the many variations on Old Glory—that have retained their power to move us even today.

The Holiday Book, then, affirms the importance of the traditions embodied in our celebrations, the days we share with family and friends and with the entire country, the days that we look forward to and remember.

In compiling The Holiday Book, my greatest debt is to my sources, acknowledged in the Selected Bibliography at the end. In addition, I am grateful for the assistance of my colleagues Peter Ferencze, Richard Rawson, and Lawrence Grow. Even they cannot possibly measure the full value of their respective contributions.

New Year's Day

The methods of reckoning the calendar and the time of beginning the year have varied greatly with different peoples and at different periods of history, but the custom of celebrating the season when the old year ended and the new year began has been universally followed from the earliest times. Few New Year's revelers in the final quarter of the twentieth century realize that the first of January has been widely accepted as the start of the year for only four centuries and that this date was fixed as the beginning of the new year quite arbitrarily.

Almost all early civilizations had reckoned time in relation to the seasons and to the positions of the sun and moon. In the arrangement of the calendar, the general practice has been to name or number the days according to their position in the month, and to name or number the months according to their position in the year. In order to do this, however, it was necessary to select a starting point for the beginning of each month and a starting point for the beginning of the year. The changes in the moon made it easy to obtain a fixed point from which to reckon the commencement of the month, but with the year it was more difficult. Which season of the year marked a true beginning? Consequently, the ancient Persians and Egyptians, for example, began their year on September 21st, the date of the autumnal equinox, and the people of ancient Greece selected the summer solstice, June 21st, as the day when their year should commence. The Romans, however, who had long celebrated the new year on March 25th, the date of the vernal equinox, were the first (153 B.C.) to initiate the year on the first of January—and they were undoubtedly the first to celebrate the day as a public event divorced from agricultural or seasonal significance.

The Romans dedicated the first month, and especially the first day, to the god Janus, and sacrifices were offered to him during the entire month. He was represented with two faces, one looking forward and the other backward, thus indicating that he stood between the old year and the new. On the first of the year all lawsuits and quarrels were suspended, differences were reconciled, and friendships renewed. The people wished each other health and prosperity; presents were given, and there was feasting, masquerading, and festivity throughout the empire.

The first Christian emperors continued these customs, but soon the Church condemned the celebrations and prohibited Christians from joining in them and finally made the first of January—eight days after Christmas—a religious festival commemorating the circumcision of Jesus. Throughout the Middle Ages, most Christians turned their backs on their Roman past by reverting to March 25th as New Year's Day, a practice ultimately ended by the adoption of the Gregorian calendar. In England, however, from whose shores so many American customs have their origin, the jovial winter celebrations were never completely abandoned.

Festivity and drinking have always been prominent features of the New Year celebration. A custom which once was generally followed was the passing around and drinking from the

Wassail cup. This was also done on Christmas and other festivals. The word is from the Anglo-Saxon and means "be whole" or "be well," and was originally a pledge drunk between friends. This was one of the prominent features of the Christmas and New Year festivities of old England. The Wassail cup was generally an elaborately ornamented bowl, often of massive silver, and was passed from one guest to another, each drinking from it in turn. The present New Year's toasts are direct successors of this ancient custom.

Another custom which was very popular in the past, particularly in Scotland, was known as "First-footing." The First-foot was the name given to the person who set foot on the threshold after the clock struck twelve. Each family made suitable preparations to receive the "First-foot." Cakes, ale, and other refreshments were served to all those who came with the intention of being the first to enter the house. The First-footers often went in parties and were always welcome to the fun and festivity, even if another visitor had in fact arrived first. In Edinburgh and other large cities of Scotland, the streets were crowded on New Year's Eve and late into the next morning with these visitors making their rounds. There were many superstitions connected with the custom, and good or bad luck was supposed to follow according to the personality of the "First-foot."

A custom somewhat resembling the "First-footing" observances was the making of New Year's calls. From the days of the earliest Dutch settlers until the middle of the nineteenth century, New Year's Day in New York and nearby cities was devoted to the making and receiving of visits. Every house was open, and it was considered a slight to omit any acquaintance when making these friendly calls. As first observed, it was a charming custom. Old friendships were renewed, family differences were settled, and a hearty welcome was extended to every visitor. Unfortunately, however, the custom was carried to excess. Gentlemen would think nothing of making seventy or eighty calls in nine or ten hours, and the ladies would compete with each other in the effort to have the greatest number of callers on New Year's Day. Gradually, the custom fell into disrepute, and, by the beginning of the twentieth century, it had all but disappeared.

The custom of watching the "old year out and new year in" is widespread and has been followed for centuries. At one time it was customary in Great Britain to unbar the house door with great formality to "let out the old year and let in the new." Many churches still hold religious services at midnight—known as "watch services"—to mark the advent of the new year. Related to this is the ringing of church bells as the old year is passing. In the early years of this century, for example, Trinity Church and other churches in New York City, and at many churches in other cities throughout the country, the chimes were rung at midnight while great crowds gathered in the streets to listen. Gradually, the noise from the celebrating crowds drowned out the chimes, leading in turn to the crowds in Times Square and in other public places that carouse and shout as the new year arrives. For the last three decades at least, millions of Americans in the electronic era have preferred to watch the Times Square merrymakers on TV, tooting horns dusted off from their last use on the previous New Year's Eve.

THE NEW YEAR

Who comes dancing over the snow,
　　His soft little feet all bare and rosy?
Open the door, though the wild winds blow,
　　Take the child in and make him cosy.
Take him in and hold him dear,
He is the wonderful glad New Year.

Dinah Maria Mulock Craik

REJOICING UPON THE
NEW YEAR'S COMING OF AGE

The Old Year being dead, and the New Year coming of age, which he does, by calendar law as soon as the breath is out of the old gentleman's body, nothing would serve the young spark but he must give a dinner upon the occasion, to which all the Days in the year were invited. The Festivals, whom he deputed as stewards, were mightily taken with the notion. They had been engaged time out of mind, they said, in providing mirth and good cheer for mortals below, and it was time they should have a taste of their own bounty.

It was stiffly debated among them whether the Fasts should be admitted. Some said the appearance of such lean, starved guests, with their mortified faces, would pervert the ends of the meeting. But the objection was overruled by Christmas Day, who had a design upon Ash Wednesday (as you shall hear), and a mighty desire to see how the old Dominie should behave himself in his cups. Only the Vigils were requested to come with their lanterns to light the gentlefolk home at night.

All the Days came. Covers were laid for three hundred and sixty-five guests at the principal table; with an occasional knife and fork at the sideboard for the Twenty-Ninth of February.

Cards of invitation had been issued. The carriers were the hours; twelve little merry whirling foot pages that went round and found out the persons invited, with the exception of Easter Day, Shrove Tuesday, and a few such movables, who had lately shifted their quarters.

Well, they all met at last, foul Days, fine Days, all sorts of Days, and a rare din they made of it. There was nothing but "Hail, fellow Day! well met!" only Lady Day seemed a little scornful. Yet some said Twelfth Day cut her out, for she came all royal and glittering and Epiphanous. The rest came in green, some in white, but Old Lent and his family were not yet out of mourning. Rainy Days came in dripping, and Sunshiny Days laughing. Wedding Days were in marriage finery. Pay Day came late, and Dooms Day sent word he might be expected.

April Fool took upon himself to marshal the guests, and May Day, with that sweetness peculiar to her, proposed the health of the host. This being done, the lordly New Year, from the upper end of the table, returned thanks. Ash Wednesday, being now called upon for a song, struck up a carol, which Christmas Day had taught him. Shrovetide, Lord Mayor's Day, and April Fool next joined in a glee, in which all the Days, chiming in, made a merry burden.

All this while Valentine's Day kept courting pretty May, who sat next him, slipping amorous *billet-doux* under the table till the Dog Days began to be jealous and to bark and rage exceedingly.

At last the Days called for their cloaks and great-coats, and took their leaves. Shortest Day went off in a deep, black fog, that wrapped the little gentleman all round. Two Vigils—so watchmen are called in Heaven—saw Christmas Day safe home; they had been used to the business before. Another Vigil—a sout, sturdy patrol, called the Eve of St. Christopher—seeing Ash Wednesday in a condition little better than he should be, e'en whipt him over his shoulders, pic-a-pack fashion, and he went floating home singing:

"On the bat's back do I fly,"

and a number of old snatches besides. Longest Day set off westward in beautiful crimson and gold; the rest, some in one fashion, some in another; but Valentine and pretty May took their departure together in one of the prettiest silvery twilights a Lover's Day could wish to set in.

Charles Lamb.

A NEW YEARS CAKE

The twelve merry Months once decided to make,
For the New Year approaching, a wonderful cake,—
Contributing freely each one, more or less,
And sharing the pride of the final success.
September, who through her acquaintance with schools
Was up in the latest grammatical rules,
Wrote out, in a lovely Spencerian hand,
A recipe any one might understand.
November,—as usual, busy and hurried,
And with her Election-cake specially worried,
For fear it would burn while her mind was so flurried,—
From what she had left on her generous hands
When her Thanksgiving cooking, with all its demands,
Was finished, the milk and the spices supplied;
While April the eggs was o'erjoyed to provide,
All colored, of course, with indelible dyes—
"My choicest!" said April, with tears in her eyes.
March furnished the sugar, and though I admit
'T was maple, still that didn't matter a bit.
He mixed the cake, too, being sturdy and stout,
And accustomed to stirring things briskly about.
The flour was from May,—her particular brand
(You've heard of the "mayflower"?), and white as her hand.
Dear June sent the flavoring,—extract of rose,
The sweetest and purest, as every one knows;
And August the butter, in cups of bright gold,
Which seemed all the sunshine of summer to hold.
February gave cherries, quite dried up and brown,
From the tree that George Washington said he cut down;
And October declared, with a laugh and a frown
(Understand, this is slang which I do not recommend!),
That to vie with his gift she could never pretend,
Though she, too, had nothing but *chestnuts* to send!
July did the baking, and skilfully, too.
'T was done top and bottom, and all the way through.
Her oven was steady and right to a T.
January's crisp icing was lovely to see.
December, quite ready to part with her best,

Declared, what with stockings and trees and the rest,

Every thing that she owned she had given away,

Save a bonbon or two and a bright holly spray.

So these, for adornment, arranged with much taste,

On the top of the beautiful structure were placed.

"Feb" dashed off a rhyme,—he was quick with his pen

From writing of valentines now and again.

And, boxed up with care, and addressed in red ink,

By the Lightning Express, which is quick as a wink

(Engaged by July), this delectable cake,

Whose like I defy any baker to bake,

Was sent New Year's morning, in triumph so clear,

From the twelve merry Months to their darling New Year.

Margaret Johnson

A NEW YEAR'S TALK

"Here I am," said the New Year, popping his head in at the door.

"Oh! there you are, eh?" replied the Old Year. "Come in, and let us have a look at you, and shut the door after you, please!"

The New Year stepped lightly in, and closed the door carefully.

"Frosty night," he said. "Fine and clear, though, I have had a delightful journey."

"Humph!" said the Old Year. "I don't expect to find it delightful, with this rheumatism racking my bones. A long, cold drive, I call it; but, to be sure, I thought it pleasant when I was your age, youngster. Is the sleigh waiting?"

"Yes," replied the other. "But there is no hurry. Wait a bit, and tell me how matters are in these parts."

"So, so!" the Old Year answered, shaking his head. "They might be better, and yet I suppose they might be worse, too. They were worse before I came; much worse, too. I have done a great deal. Now I expect you, my boy, to follow my example, and be a good year all the way through."

"I shall do my best," said the New Year, "depend upon it! And now tell me a little what there is to do."

"In the first place," replied the other, "you have the weather to attend to. To be sure, you have a clerk to help you in that, but he is not always to be depended upon, there is a great deal of work in the department. The seasons have a way of running into each other, and getting mixed, if you don't keep a sharp lookout on them; and the months are a troublesome, unruly set. Then you must be careful how you turn on wet and dry weather; your reputation depends a great measure on that. And one thing I want you to do very carefully; that is, to watch the leaves that are turned."

"I thought Autumn attended to that sort of thing," said his companion.

"I don't mean leaves of trees," said the Old Year. "But at the beginning of a year, half the people in the world say, 'I am going to turn over a new leaf!' meaning that they intend to behave themselves better in various respects. As a rule, leaves do not stay turned over. I know a great many little boys who promised me to turn over a new leaf in regard to tearing their clothes, and losing their jack-knives, and bringing mud into the house on their boots, and little girls who were going to keep their bureau drawers tidy and their boot buttons sewed on. But I haven't seen much improvement in most of them."

"I'll attend to it," said the New Year. "Any suggestions?"

"Well," said the Old Year, smiling. "I have never found that young people, or young years, were very apt to profit by good advice. You must go your own way after all. Don't start any new inventions—there have been quite enough lately. Above all, take care of the children, and give them all the good weather you can conscientiously. And now," he added, rising slowly and stiffly from his seat by the fire, "the horses are getting impatient, and my time is nearly up, so I start on my long drive. You will find everything in pretty good shape, I think, though, of course, you will think me an old fogy, as perhaps I am. Well! well! good-bye, my boy! Good luck to you!"

Laura E. Richards

THE TWO ROADS

It was New Year's night. An aged man was standing at a window. He mournfully raised his eyes towards the deep blue sky, where the stars were floating like white lilies on the surface of a clear, calm lake. Then he cast them on the earth, where few more helpless beings than himself were moving towards their inevitable goal—the tomb. Already he had passed sixty of the stages which lead to it, and he had brought from his journey nothing but errors and remorse. His health was destroyed, his mind unfurnished, his heart sorrowful, and his old age devoid of comfort.

The days of his youth rose up in a vision before him, and he recalled the solemn moment when his father had placed him at the entrance of two roads, one leading into a peaceful, sunny land, covered with a fertile harvest, and resounding with soft, sweet songs; while the other conducted the wanderer into a deep, dark cave, whence there was no issue, where poison flowed instead of water, and where serpents hissed and crawled.

He looked towards the sky, and cried out, in his anguish: "O youth, return! O my father, place me once more at the crossway of life, that I may choose the better road!" But the days of his youth had passed away, and his parents were with the departed. He saw wandering lights float over dark marshes, and then disappear. "Such," he said, "were the days of my wasted life!" he exclaimed; and the sharp arrows of unavailing remorse struck him to the heart.

Then he remembered his early companions, who had entered life with him, but who having trod the paths of virtue and industry, were now happy and honored on this New Year's night. The clock in the high church-tower struck, and the sound, falling on his ear, recalled the many tokens of the love of his parents for him, their erring son; the lessons they had taught him; the prayers they had offered up in his behalf. Overwhelmed with shame and grief, he dared no longer look towards that heaven where they dwelt. His darkened eyes dropped tears, and, with one despairing effort, he cried aloud, "Come back, my early days! Come back!"

And his youth *did* return; for all this had been but a dream, visiting his slumbers on New Year's night. He was still young; his errors only were no dream. He thanked God fervently that time was still his own; that he had not yet entered the deep, dark cavern, but that he was free to tread the road leading to the peaceful land where sunny harvests wave.

Ye who still linger on the threshold of life, doubting which path to choose, remember that when years shall be passed, and your feet shall stumble on the dark mountain, you will cry bitterly, but cry in vain, "O youth, return! O, give me back my early days!"

Jean Paul Richter

THE CHILD AND THE YEAR

Said the child to the youthful year:
    "What hast thou in store for me,
O giver of beautiful gifts! what cheer,
    What joy dost thou bring with thee?"

"My seasons four shall bring
    Their treasures: the winter's snows,
The autumn's store, and the flowers of spring,
    And the summer's perfect rose.

"All these and more shall be thine,
    Dear child—but the last and best
Thyself must earn by a strife divine,
    If thou wouldst be truly blest.

"Wouldst know this last, best gift?
    'Tis a conscience clear and bright,
A peace of mind which the soul can lift
    To an infinite delight.

"Truth, patience, courage, and love,
    If thou unto me canst bring,
I will set thee all earth's ills above,
    O child! and crown thee a king!"

Celia Thaxter

Lincoln's Birthday

Abraham Lincoln's humble origins and tragic end place him at the head of the assembly of American heroes. Within a year after his assassination on Good Friday, April 14, 1865, national figures were calling for the commemoration of his birth. And by the end of the 1800s, this day was an official holiday in all of the states of the North and in a few south of the Mason-Dixon line. Now—over one hundred years after the deep division and bitterness of the Civil War—February 12th is a true national holiday shared by Northerners and Southerners, Republicans and Democrats.

Lincoln was born in Kentucky on February 12, 1809, and was one of the few American presidents who could claim honestly to have been born in a log cabin. His ancestors had settled in Massachusetts in 1638, and like many other Americans of the time, were soon to begin the move West. Kentucky was just one stop in the long trek in search of prosperity and peace of mind. By 1816, the family moved to Spencer County, Indiana, and fourteen years later, when Abraham Lincoln was 21, they made their final settlement in central Illinois. Thus, although Lincoln was a Midwesterner—and gave every evidence of such regional upbringing in his appearance and manner—he was also a man of strong New England character and of border Southern temperament. This became more and more evident as his career in public service developed through the 1840s and '50s.

Today visitors to New Salem State Park and Springfield, Illinois, can gain some sense of what life was like at the time. This was still frontier country, and money was scarce. Men and women were largely self-taught, and the Bible was read as history, theology, and philosophy. Lincoln claimed no religious denomination as his own, but his thoughts and words were to be shaped by the noble language and humanitarian principles to be found in the King James Version of the Bible. His life was also enriched by the lively oral story-telling tradition of country living. He was a man adept with words, able to put people at ease with familiar but instructive tales of the backwoods variety. In the 1830s the study of law was begun, and this was combined with service in the Illinois state legislature. By 1846 he reached Washington for the first time as a United States Representative, and his winning and thoughtful manner quickly brought him to the attention of prominent politicians throughout the country. When the Republican party was being formed in the late 1850s on the ruins of the old Whig party, Lincoln was seen as a logical candidate for higher office. In 1858 he made a try for the United States Senate, but was defeated by Stephen A. Douglas, the Democratic candidate. The contest—and its series of famous debates over that most crucial of issues, slavery—made the name of Lincoln a household word everywhere in the country. The Republicans naturally turned to him in 1860 to carry the party's banner against two Democrats leading different divisions of the party, as well as a Union party candidate.

Only a month after his inauguration as president on March 4, 1861, Lincoln was forced to deal militarily with the crisis of secession. The underlying issue was, of course, the question of slavery and its abolition. But the immediate cause of conflict was the principle of states rights, the sovereignty of the national government over the state. Abolition of slavery or emancipation of black men, women, and children was not to occur for another two and a half years. Lincoln had a mystical devotion to the Union, and in his famous speech of June, 1858, this philosophy was perfectly expressed: "A house divided against itself cannot stand. I believe this government cannot endure permanently half slave and half free. I do not expect the Union to be dissolved—I do not expect the house to fall—but I do expect it will cease to be divided. It will become all one thing, or all the other. Either the opponents of slavery will arrest the further spread of it, and place it where the public mind shall rest in the belief that it is in the course of ultimate extinction; or its advocates will push it forward till it shall become alike lawful in all the states, old as well as new, North as well as South."

No president has so loathed war. And neither has any president before or since been resolved to see that it be waged as humanely as humanly possible. Lincoln was not an abolitionist. But neither was he blind to the disgrace and degradation of slavery. In his own words: "As I would not be a slave, so I would not be a master. This expresses my idea of democracy. Whatever differs from this, to the extent of the difference, is no democracy."

The political and military situation during the terrible war was complex and exhausting, but the basic issue was kept clear by Lincoln. It was to bring to life the very principles of American democracy, to extend the Bill of Rights to all. And there could never be a solution to these fatal flaws in the body politic without the political framework of one nation, one constitution, one people. Permanent division would mean only continued bloodshed and suffering for white and black alike.

Throughout the war years of 1861–1865, Lincoln preached peace and conciliation. While directing the military course of the conflict as Commander-in-Chief, he sought always—from the White House to Gettysburg—the healing of wounds. When the end came at Appomattox, on April 9, 1865, Lincoln was grateful rather than jubilant. His deeply lined face was evidence enough of the emotional fatigue of the war; his lanky 6'4" frame, photographs of the time show, was now stooped. The young "railsplitter" from the Midwest had become, in the eyes of truly free men everywhere, "Father Abraham," the "Great Emancipator."

With his death five days after bringing the Union together again, the figure of Lincoln assumed its apotheosis, a magnetic mythical stature. Coming as it did in the holiest week of the Christian year, the crazed crime of John Wilkes Booth unleased one of the most moving and dramatic of national demonstrations of public grief. Not until the death of John F. Kennedy would America be so demonstrably moved by the loss of a public person. The greatest of America's poets, Walt Whitman, expressed the very best of this sentiment in words that will last as long as the memory of the great man:

> When lilacs last in the dooryard bloom'd
> And the great star early droop'd in the western sky in the night,
> I mourn'd, and yet shall mourn with ever-returning spring.
> Ever-returning spring, trinity sure to me you bring,
> Lilac blooming perennial and drooping star in the west,
> And thought of him I love.

SAYINGS OF LINCOLN

Gold is good in its place; but living, brave, and patriotic men are better than gold.

Where slavery is, there liberty cannot be; and where liberty is, there slavery cannot be.

With malice toward none, with charity for all, with firmness in the right, as God gives us to see the right.—*From the Second Inaugural Address*

All that I am, or hope to be, I owe to my angel mother.

It is better only sometimes to be right than at all times to be wrong.

I do not wish to die until the world is better for my having lived.

When I am dead I wish my friends to remember that I always plucked a thistle and planted a rose when in my power.

Those who deny freedom to others deserve it not for themselves, and under a just God cannot retain it.

If we do right God will be with us and if God is with us we cannot fail.

He who does something at the head of one regiment will eclipse him who does nothing at the head of a hundred.

LINCOLN'S PERSONAL APPEARANCE

Lincoln's personal appearance is thus described by Joseph H. Choate as he saw him in 1860:
"He appeared in every sense of the word like one of the plain people among whom he loved to be counted.
At first sight there was nothing impressive or imposing about him except his great stature
which singled him out from the crowd; his clothes hung awkwardly on his giant frame;
his face was that of a dark pallor, without the slightest tinge of color;
his seamed and rugged features bore the furrows of hardship and struggle;
his deep-set eyes looked sad and anxious; his countenance in repose gave little evidence
of that brain power which had raised him from the lowest to the highest station among his countrymen;
as he talked to me before the meeting he seemed ill at ease, with that sort of apprehension
which a young man might feel before presenting himself to a new and strange audience."

Lincoln described himself thus: "I am, in height, six feet four inches nearly;
lean in flesh, weighing on an average one hundred and eighty pounds; dark complexion,
with coarse black hair and gray eyes.
No other marks or brands recollected."

YOUNG LINCOLN

Men saw no portents on that night
A hundred years ago. No omens flared
Above that rail-built cabin with one door,
And windowless to all the peering stars.
They laid him in the hollow of a log,
Humblest of cradles, save the other one—
The manger in the stall at Bethlehem.

No portents! yet with whisper and alarm
The Evil Powers that dread the nearing feet
Of heroes held a council in that hour;
And sent three fates to darken that low door
To baffle and beat back the heaven-sent child.
Three were the fates—gaunt Poverty that chains,
Gray Drudgery that grinds the hope away,
And gaping Ignorance that starves the soul.

They came with secret laughters to destroy.
Ever they dogged him, counting every step,
Waylaid his youth and struggled for his life.
They came to master, but he made them serve.
And from the wrestle with the destinies,
He rose with all his energies aglow.

For God, upon whose steadfast shoulders rest
These governments of ours, had not forgot.
He needed for His purposes a voice,
A voice to be a clarion on the wind,
Crying the word of freedom to dead hearts,
The word the centuries had waited for.

So hidden in the West, God shaped His Man.
There in the unspoiled solitudes he grew,
Unwarped by culture and uncramped by creed;
Keeping his course courageous and alone,
As goes the Mississippi to the sea.
His daring spirt burst the narrow bounds,
Rose resolute; and like the sea-called stream,
He tore new channels where he found no way.

The tools were his first teachers, sternly kind.
The plow, the scythe, the maul, the echoing axe,

Taught him their homely wisdom and their peace.
He had the plain man's genius—common sense,
Yet rage for knowledge drove his mind afar;
He fed his spirit with the bread of books,
And slaked his thirst at all the wells of thought.

But most he read the heart of common man,
Scanned all its secret pages stained with tears,
Saw all the guile, saw all the piteous pain;
And yet could keep the smile about his lips,
Love and forgive, see all and pardon all;
His only fault, the fault that some of old
Laid even on God—that he was ever wont
To bend the law to let his mercy out.

Edwin Markham

LINCOLN'S HUMANITY

No custodian of absolute power ever exercised it so benignly as did Abraham Lincoln. His interposition in behalf of men sentenced to death by court-martial became so demoralizing that his generals in the field united in a round-robin protest. Both Grant and Sherman cut the wires between army headquarters and the White House to escape his interference with the iron rule of military discipline.

A characteristic story is told by John B. Ally, of Boston, who, going to the White House three days in succession found each day in one of the outer halls a gray-haired old man, silently weeping. The third day, touched by this not incommon spectacle, he went up to the old man and ascertained that he had a son under sentence of death, and was trying to reach the President.

"Come along," said Ally, "I'll take you to the President."

Mr. Lincoln listened to the old man's pitiful story, and then sadly replied that he had just received a telegram from the general commanding imploring him not to interfere. The old man cast one last heart-broken look at the President, and started shuffing toward the door. Before he reached it, Mr. Lincoln called him back.

"Come back, old man," he said, "Come back! The generals may telegraph and telegraph, but I am going to pardon that young man."

Thereupon he sent a despatch directing sentence to be suspended until execution should be ordered by himself. Then the old man burst out crying again.

"Mr. Lincoln," said he, "that is not a pardon; you only hold up the sentence of my boy until you can order him to be shot!"

Lincoln turned quickly and, half smiles, half tears, replied, "Go along, old man, go along in peace; if your boy lives until I order him to be shot, he'll grow to be as old as Methuselah."

Henry Watterson.

THE MAN OF PEACE

What winter holiday is this?
  In Time's great calendar,
Marked with the rubric of the saints,
  And with a soldier's star,
Here stands the name of one who lived
  To serve the common weal,
With humor, tender as a prayer,
  And honor firm as steel.

No hundred hundred years can dim
  The radiance of his birth,
That set unselfish laughter free
  From all the suns of earth.
Unswerved through stress and scant success,
  Out of his dreamful youth
He kept an unperverted faith
  In the almighty truth.

Born in the fulness of the days,
  Up from the teeming soil,
By the world-mother reared and schooled
  In reverence and toil,
He stands the test of all life's best

  Through play, defeat, or strain;
Never a moment was he found
  Unlovable or vain.

Fondly we set apart this day,
  And mark this plot of earth
To be forever hallowed ground
  In honor of his birth,
Where men may come as to a shrine
  And temple of the good,
To be made sweet and srong of heart
  In Lincoln's brotherhood. . . .

Bliss Carman

THE GETTYSBURG ADDRESS

Fourscore and seven years ago, our fathers brought forth upon this continent a new nation, conceived in liberty, and dedicated to the proposition that all men are created equal. Now we are engaged in a great civil war, testing whether that nation, or any nation so conceived and so dedicated, can long endure. We are met on a great battle-field of that war. We have come to dedicate a portion of that field as a final resting-place for those who here gave their lives that that nation might live. It is altogether fitting and proper that we should do this. But in a larger sense we cannot dedicate, we cannot consecrate, we cannot hallow this ground. The brave men living and dead, who struggled here, have consecrated it far above our power to add or detract. The world will little note nor long remember what we say here, but it can never forget what they did here. It is for us, the living, rather to be dedicated here to the unfinished work which they who fought here have thus far so nobly advanced. It is rather for us to be here dedicated to the great task remaining before us, that from these honored dead we take increased devotion to that cause for which they gave the last full measure of devotion; that we here highly resolve that these dead shall not have died in vain; that this nation, under God, shall have a new birth of freedom, and that government of the people, by the people, and for the people, shall not perish from the earth.

Abraham Lincoln.

November 19, 1863.

THE DEATH OF LINCOLN

Never did two such orbs of experience meet in one hemisphere, as the joy and the sorrow of the same week in this land. The joy of final victory was as sudden as if no man had expected it, and as entrancing as if it had fallen a sphere from heaven. It rose up over sobriety, and swept business from its moorings, and ran down through the land in irresistible course. Men embraced each other in brotherhood that were strangers in the flesh. They sang, or prayed, or, deeper yet, many could only think thanksgiving and weep gladness.

In one hour, under the blow of a single bereavement, joy lay without a pulse, without a gleam, or breath. A sorrow came that swept through the land as huge storms through the forest and field, rolling thunder along the sky, disheveling the flowers, daunting every singer in thicket and forest, and pouring blackness and darkness across the land and upon the mountains. Did ever so many hearts, in so brief a time, touch two such boundless feelings? It was the uttermost of joy; it was the uttermost of sorrow— noon and midnight without a space between.

And now the martyr is moving in triumphal march, mightier than when alive. The nation rises up at every stage of his coming. Cities and States are his pall-bearers, and the cannon beats the hours with solemn progression. Dead—dead—dead—he yet speaketh!

Is Washington dead? Is Hampton dead? Is David dead? Is any man dead that ever was fit to live?

Disenthralled of flesh, and risen to the unobstructed sphere where passion never comes, he begins his illimitable work. His life now is grafted upon the Infinite, and will be fruitful as no earthly life can be.

Pass on, thou that hast overcome! Your sorrows, O people, are his peace! Your bells, and bands, and muffled drums sound triumph in his ear. Wail and weep here: God makes it joy and triumph there. Pass on, thou victor!

Henry Ward Beecher.

Discourse at Plymouth Church on Sunday after Lincoln's Assassination.

O CAPTAIN! MY CAPTAIN!

O Captain! my Captain! our fearful trip is done,
The ship has weather'd every rack, the prize we sought is won,
The port is near, the bells I hear, the people all exulting,
While follow eyes the steady keel, the vessel grim and daring;
 But O heart! heart! heart!
  O the bleeding drops of red,
 Where on the deck my Captain lies,
  Fallen cold and dead.

O Captain! my Captain! rise up and hear the bells;
Rise up—for you the flag is flung—for you the bugle trills,
For you bouquets and ribbon'd wreaths—for you the shores a-crowding,
For you they call, the swaying mass, their eager faces turning;
 Here Captain! dear father!
  This arm beneath your head!
 It is some dream that on the deck
  You've fallen cold and dead.

My Captain does not answer, his lips are pale and still,
My father does not feel my arm, he has no pulse nor will,
The ship is anchored safe and sound, its voyage closed and done,
From fearful trip the victor ship comes in with object won;
 Exult O shores, and ring O bells!
  But I with mournful tread,
 Walk the deck my Captain lies,
  Fallen cold and dead.

Walt Whitman

LINCOLN'S CHARACTER

Lincoln was the purest, the most generous, the most magnanimous of men.

General W. T. Sherman

Such a life and character will be treasured forever as the sacred possession of the American people and of mankind.

James A. Garfield

His career teaches young men that every position of eminence is open before the diligent and worthy.

Bishop Matthew Simpson

His constant thought was his country and how to serve it.

Charles Sumner

He knew no fear except the fear of doing wrong.

Robert G. Ingersoll

Abraham Lincoln leaves for America's history and biography, so far, not only its most dramatic reminiscence—he leaves in my opinion the greatest, best, most characteristic, artistic, and moral personality.

Walt Whitman

St. Valentine's Day

St. Valentine's Day, the 14th of February, is the anniversary of the death of St. Valentine, a martyr of the early Christian Church, but it is better known as the day on which people exchange messages of love and sentiment.

St. Valentine was a Roman bishop who remained steadfast to the Christian faith during the persecution under the Emperor Claudius, and for this he was cast into prison and subsequently beheaded. While in prison he is said to have cured the jailer's daughter of blindness. His martyrdom is supposed to have taken place on February 14th, about the year 270.

St. Valentine's anniversary is now, however, principally observed as a day for the exchange of love messages and tokens of sentiment. The origin of this custom is shrouded in mystery, for there is nothing in the life of the Saint to which any such observance can be traced. One explanation, rooted in tradition, is that the birds begin to mate on this date, and the practice of young people choosing their "valentines" on that day originated from this idea. Another explanation is that the Norman word *galatin,* meaning a lover, was often written and pronounced *valentin,* and through a natural confusion of names, St. Valentine became the patron saint of lovers. As to birds choosing their mates on February 14th, Chaucer in his *Parliament of Foules* refers to the belief in this manner:

For this was Seynt Valentyne's day,
When every foul cometh ther to choose his mate.

And, in a seventeeth-century poem, John Donne elaborates upon the same idea:

Hail, Bishop Valentine! whose day this is;
All the air is thy diocese,
And all the chirping choristers
And other birds are thy parishioners:
Thou marryest every year
The lyric lark and the grave whispering dove;
The sparrow that neglects his life for love,
The household bird with the red stomacher;
Thou mak'st the blackbird speed as soon,
As doth the goldfinch or the halcyon. . . .
This day more cheerfully than ever shine,
This day which might inflame thyself, old Valentine!

It is also said that in ancient Persia a festival was celebrated in February, called the "Merd-giran" in honor of the angel who was deemed the special guardian for women. On this occasion women enjoyed the privilege of absolute power. The husband obeyed all the commands of his wife, and the unmarried women, without offense to decorum, were permitted to pay court to whom they pleased. A similar custom existed for centuries in Europe on the 14th of February, when it was not considered "indelicate" for a young woman to pay addresses to any man she favored.

The most probable explanation, however, and the one most generally accepted, is that the observance of Valentine's Day was a survival of the old Roman festival of the "Lupercalia," which was celebrated about the 15th of February in honor of Pan, the god of shepherds and country people, and Juno, the goddess of marriage and the guardian of women. At this festival, among other ceremonies, it was the custom to put the names of young women into a box, these names being drawn as lots by the men as chance directed. This custom of choosing partners continued after the advent of Christianity, and it is believed that since the time of the ceremony was also the anniversary of St. Valentine, those so chosen naturally came to be called "Valentines." Whatever its origin, the custom was common in France and England for centuries. In the sixteenth century, St. Francis de Salis tried to suppress this survival of paganism by substituting saints' names in place of those of girls. The boys drew and were supposed to imitate the virtues of the saint named. But, understandably, this did not meet with much success, and the young people soon went back to the old custom.

In England the custom was that the couple so chosen would be partners for the day, or for several days, but the bond often lasted for life, as there was a certain superstitious regard for this chance selection; and while the selection was not binding, the influence of association and superstition often made it so. In France the sentimental bond caused by this chance selection was expected to last for one year, during which period the couple bore the relation of Cavalier and Lady of Beauty, the Knight being bound to the honor and defence of the Lady, for which she repaid him with smiles and favors. In Scotland, and sometimes in other countries, the "valentine" was the first young man or woman that one chanced to meet on the street or anywhere. Of this custom, John Gay wrote:

Last Valentine, the day when birds of kind
Their paramours with mutual chirpings find,
I early rose, just at the break of day,
Before the sun had chas'd the stars away:
Afield I went, amid the morning dew,
To milk my kine (for so should house-wives do.)
Thee first I spied, and the first swain we see,
In spite of Fortune, shall our true love be.

It was at one time the custom for the young man or woman to challenge his or her "valentine." This challenge consisted simply in saying, "Good Morrow, 'tis St. Valentine's Day," and he or she who said it first on meeting a person of the opposite sex received a present. Later the custom was that a gentleman alone should give the present, but only if he were successfully challenged by a young woman.

Today, of course, the 14th of February is marked almost entirely by the exchange of cards, sentimental or comic, called *valentines*. The origin of the valentine is discussed elsewhere in this chapter.

VALENTINES

Little is known as to the origin of the written or printed love message or valentine which is about the only custom of the day which is still observed. It is said that the earliest examples of poetical valentines were written in the Tower of London, by Charles, Duke of Orleans, who was taken prisoner at the battle of Agincourt in 1415. These are preserved among the manuscripts in the British Museum.

The first record that is found of a picture or drawing in connection with the day is in Pepys' Diary in the year 1667. In this book mention is made of the name being written in fancy gold letters on blue paper. In another instance the name is accompanied by a motto. Something like this is probably the origin of the modern valentine. It was an easy step to combine the illustration and the motto or some sentimental verse and allow the sender unlimited choice as to whom it might be sent. Exactly when this method was introduced is not known, but by the beginning of the 19th century the custom was fully established.

At first these valentines were all made by the hand of the sender and the elaborateness of the design and the beauty of the sentiment must have been largely governed by his or her artistic and literary ability. The verses, which were one of the most popular features of the valentine, soon became the easiest part of the message, for the writer could refer to some of the numerous little books of sentimental verses issued especially for his assistance. The first book of this kind was printed in 1797 and many others soon followed. The titles of some of them were the "Gentleman's New Valentine Writer," "Bower of Cupid," "Cupid's Annual Charter," etc. There was one designed especially for ladies called the "Ladies' Polite Valentine Writer." There were also special books for the trades-people, providing suitable valentine verses for almost every known trade and profession. There was also one for the joker called "Quizzing Valentine Writer."

The use of these little manuals, however, was not long lived, for about 1800 the first manufactured valentines made their appearance and soon took the place of the homemade article. With the introduction of cheap postage and the reduction in the cost of printing, the manufactured valentine became very popular and the sending of valentines reached its height about the middle of the 19th century.

These manufactured valentines ranged from the plain little sheet with its crude woodcut and motto costing a few pennies, to the elaborate and costly productions of silver and gilt, artificial flowers and lace paper, made so they would unfold again and again with a fresh sentiment or message at each turn. The cheap comic valentines with their hideous and vulgar colored pictures are of comparatively recent date and fortunately are falling into disuse.

Anonymous, 1913

A VALENTINE

I stood at Rimmel's window, and I saw that there were signs
That the festival approaching was the bold St. Valentine's;
There were lots of little Cupids in a cloud of dainty lace,
They were podgy in the stomach, they were chubby in the face!
And a dicky-bird I noticed, in its beak a little ring,
Just the bird to drop the present in a lady's hand and sing.
Then I suddenly remembered that the worthy Mrs. D.
Last year had very kindly sent a valentine to me,
So I stepped up to the counter, and a smiling maiden brought
All the best of the collection, thinking one of them I sought.
"For a sweetheart," said she, coyly, "here's a beautiful design;"
'Twas a fan with painted roses, and the legend, "I am thine,"
"No, it isn't for a sweetheart, but my wife," I shyly said.
Back that damsel put the boxes, and she tossed her little head,
Crying, "Oh, I beg your pardon!" while she smiled at the mistake;
"*That's* the sort of thing you want, sir—*it's the cheapest one we make.*"

—*George R. Sims.*

ST. VALENTINE'S DAY
CUSTOMS AND SUPERSTITIONS

St. Valentine's Day was formerly considered as having superstitious significance and many charms and divinations were connected with the day. Catching a lover asleep on this morning was looked upon as prophetic of good luck, and that the course of true love would run smooth. Sometimes the girls would write the names of those who might be their valentines on slips of paper, roll them in clay and put them in water. The first to rise was to be the favored one.

Another charm was to find out whether they would be married within the year. To do this the girl would obtain five bay leaves, and pin them on her pillow, one at each corner and one in the centre. If she dreamt of her sweetheart they would be married within the year. To make the charm more certain the girl would sometimes take a hard boiled egg, remove the yolk, then eat it shell and all and go straight to bed without speaking or drinking.

A pretty way of celebrating the day, which is still observed in some English villages, is called "Valentining." The children gather in a little band in the morning and go from house to house singing some little chorus, and are given in return pennies or candies.

Anonymous, 1913

A VALENTINE

Accept, dear wife, this little token,
   And, if between the lines you seek,
You'll find the love I've often spoken—
   The love I always love to speak.

Our little ones are making merry
   With unco ditties rhymed in jest;
But in these lines, though awkward, very,
   The genuine article's expressed!

You are as fair and sweet and tender,
   Dear, brown-eyed little sweetheart mine,
As when a callow youth and slender,
   I asked to be your valentine.

What though these years of ours be fleeting?
   What though the years of youth be flown?
I'll mock old Kronos with repeating:
   "I love my love and her alone!"

And when I fall before His reaping,
   And when my stuttering speech is done,
Think not my love is dead or sleeping,
   But that it waits for you to come.

So take, dear love, this little token,
   And if there speaks in any line
The sentiment I'll fain have spoken,
   Say, will you kiss your valentine?

—*Eugene Field.*

VALENTINES TO MY MOTHER

1880

More shower than shine
Brings sweet St. Valentine;
Warm shine, warm shower,
Bring up sweet flower on flower.

Through shower and shine
Loves you your Valentine,
Through shine, through shower,
Through summer's flush,
Through autumn's fading hour.

1885

All the Robin Redbreasts
   Have lived the winter through,
Jenny Wrens have pecked their fill
   And found a work to do;
Families of Sparrows
   Have weathered wind and storm
With Rabbit on the stony hill
   And Hare upon her form.

You and I, my Mother,
   Have lived the winter through,
And still we play our daily parts
   And still find work to do;
And still the cornfields flourish,
   The olive and the vine,
And till you reign my Queen of Hearts
   And I'm your Valentine.

Christina Georgina Rossetti

ARRIVAL OF THE COUNTRY POSTMAN ON ST. VALENTINE'S MORNING.

TO ST. VALENTINE

St. Valentine, though wide your fame,
You don't deserve your pious name,
And this the reason of my plaint—
Your conduct misbefits a saint.

From youth-time up to middle age
I've catered for your patronage,
But ever since we've been acquaint
You haven't acted like a saint.

For when comes round, as fixed as fate,
The day which you appropriate,
You give me cause for new complaint
In manner most unlike a saint. . . .

Your halo's rimmed with many a dart;
Your symbol is a wounded heart;
Fond swains you lure with artful feint;
Such actions don't become a saint.

Your name no longer should appear
In saintly calendar 'tis clear,
For I affirm, without restraint,
You're more a sinner than a saint.

Jennie Betts Hartswick

VALENTINE VERSES

My patron saint, St. Valentine,
Why dost thou leave me to repine,
Still supplicating at her shrine?

But bid her eyes to me incline—
I'll ask no other sun to shine—
More rich than is Golconda's mine.

Range all that woman, song, or wine
Can give; wealth, power, and fame combine,—
For her I'd gladly all resign.

Take all the pearls are in the brine,
Sift heaven for stars; earth's flowers entwine—
But be her heart my Valentine.

Thomas Nelson Page

VALENTINE TO
A MAN OF WORTH

Fair Sir! to you my maiden intuitions—
  Shy, but sincere—ingenuously incline,
And if I find you answer the conditions,
  I'll take your bid and be your Valentine.

I know your worth—that is, your general merit;
  But, when your mourned and wealthy father died,
Pray tell a simple girl, did you inherit
  His virtues only—or—a bit beside?

Yes, I admire your lofty reputation,
  Dear to my artless spirit as my own;
But tell me this—to still my trepidation—
  Are you an owner in Bell Telephone?

Your learning, too, has bound my heart in fetters—
  For you are wise, if street report be true;
I, too, a childish fancy have for letters—
  I hope you're solid on "C. B. & Q."

Your noble presence—"dignified and stately"—
  With inexperienced ardor I adore;
But those Villard stocks! Have you tried 'em lately?
  And were you long or short on that Lake Shore?

So, gentle Sir, if you aright but read me,
  And will with all your Bonds and Stocks be mine,
Then into Mutual Union you shall lead me,
  And I will be—
            Your booming Valentine

—*Edward A. Church*

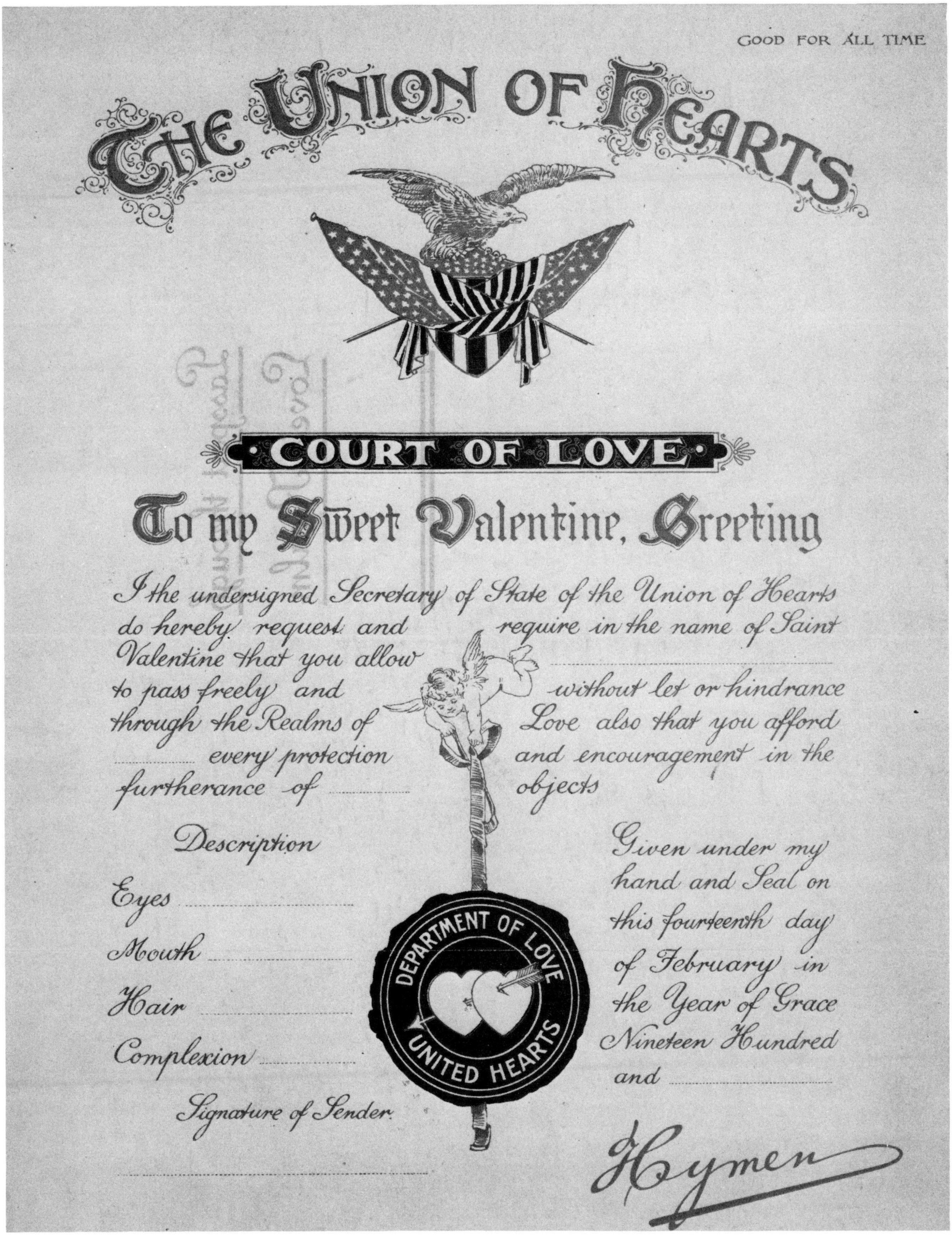

47

THE UNION OF HEARTS

· COURT OF LOVE ·

To my Sweet Valentine, Greeting

I the undersigned Secretary of State of the Union of Hearts do hereby request and require in the name of Saint Valentine that you allow _____ to pass freely and without let or hindrance through the Realms of Love also that you afford _____ every protection and encouragement in the furtherance of _____ objects

Description

Eyes _____

Mouth _____

Hair _____

Complexion _____

Signature of Sender

_____

Given under my hand and Seal on this fourteenth day of February in the Year of Grace Nineteen Hundred and _____

Hymen

DEPARTMENT OF LOVE
UNITED HEARTS

Washington's Birthday

The figure of George Washington has survived to this day as the most important and illustrious of Americans. Despite various attempts to gild his image with apocryphal stories of youthful virtue, Washington remains a man of great nobility and simple strength. Even in his own lifetime, the "Father of Our Country" found it necessary to discourage the pretensions of his fervent supporters. There were those who would have made him a king, "His Excellency" rather than "Mr. President." What he could not discourage, however, were celebrations of the day of his birth—February 22nd. These were begun as early as the late 1770s on the battlefields of the Revolution. By the time of his death on December 14, 1799, observance of the birthday was in the process of becoming a national holiday, and has been so celebrated on American territory everywhere since the late 19th century.

Thomas Jefferson, not one of Washington's most devoted friends, provided a particularly good summation of this great man's strengths:

His mind was great and powerful, without being of the very first order; his penetration strong, though not so acute as that of a Newton, Bacon, or Locke; and as far as he saw, no judgment was ever sounder. It was slow in operation, being little aided by invention or imagination, but sure in conclusion. . . . His integrity was most pure, his justice the most inflexible I have ever known. . . . He was indeed, in every sense of the words, a wise, a good and a great man. . . . On the whole, his character was, in its mass, perfect, in nothing bad, in few points indifferent; and it may truly be said, that never did nature and fortune combine more perfectly to make a man great, and to place him in the same constellation with whatever worthies have merited from man an everlasting remembrance.

This view is a great deal more valuable, though less evocative, than that first provided by Parson Mason Locke Weems in 1800 in an 80-page biography. Parson Weems's *Life of George Washington* went through many editions during the 19th century and is the source for the several popular legends of the young Washington, including the cherry tree tale and that of tossing a coin across the Rappahannock River. It is now hard to imagine Washington's birthday without replicas of the tree, models of the hatchet he used to chop down the fated cherry, or, even red cherries. And there is no reason why the model of the truthful youth should not be held up for the admiration of children everywhere. The full strength of the man, however, only emerges with a consideration of his very human qualities.

Washington was a horseman, perhaps more comfortable riding across the fields of his plantation home, Mount Vernon, or through the forests of the Shenandoah Valley than plodding along the streets of New York or Philadelphia—the first capitals of the new United States—by foot. In fact, the lurching gait of the elderly Washington was unsteady at best. Astride a horse, he was fully the Commander-in-Chief of the Revolutionary forces, the dignified and sagacious chief executive of his country, the successful gentleman farmer. By the time he was sixteen, the youthful Virginian had traveled by horseback to the back country to survey lands for Lord Fairfax. During the French and Indian War of 1754 to 1763, Washington was found by the British to be an indispensable guide, and, eventually, field commander. He was truly at home on the frontier and with frontiersmen who were determined to save the West for the English colonists. Only a love for his family home and the pursuit of agricultural interests would draw him away from the rough-and-ready life of the frontier.

Washington was a farmer. "Agriculture," he wrote, "is the most healthful, most useful, and most noble employment of man." Although by no means a dirt farmer—Washington was a slave-owner who provided for the freeing of his slaves on his death—he was a man deeply interested in the methods of producing abundant crops, in this case, flax and tobacco. Although a figure of considerable physical vitality, his features were by no means those of a fine aristocrat. Gilbert Stuart, the most famous of Washington's portrait artists, wrote in 1797, "There are features in his face totally different from what I ever observed in that of any other human being; the sockets of the eyes, for instance, are larger, and the upper part of the nose broader." "Yet," Stuart added, "his judgment and great self-command make him appear a man of a different cast in the eyes of the world." Then there was the matter of teeth, a sensitive subject to consider. Wahington's adopted son, George Washington Parke Custis, noted that "In 1789 the first president lost all his teeth." This is painfully obvious in many of the late renderings. In common with many other men of the time, Washington had to be fitted with a wooden apparatus which disfigured his face. How much the President must have disliked the ceremonial occasions which required great social presence. It was surely with great relief that he returned in 1797—after two terms as President—to Virginia and farming.

Washington was, above all, a devoted citizen and public servant. He was a churchman, a Church of England man who attempted to live by the rules of the Bible and the Book of Common Prayer. He was a country squire who naturally assumed responsibility for others. His instinctive sense of authority and justice made him the perfect leader of men. If he had been born in England—as had his ancestors—he would undoubtedly have been sent to the House of Commons by his home county. Washington, however, was a true colonist. He had no desire to hobnob with the wealthy and illustrious of London or the Continent. Although he enjoyed possessing luxurious goods from the sophisticated centers of European culture and even fine china from the Far East, his own style of living differed greatly from that of Franklin or Jefferson. His sense of civic duty led him to the corridors of power, and it was simple for him to decline serving a third term as President, to resist the flattery of those seeking favor. By turning the reins of power over to a freely elected successor, he established a tradition of proper constitutional responsibility which nourished the roots of American democracy.

The towering obelisk on the Mall in Washington—finally completed after 37 years of off-and-on construction in 1885—stands as the most prominent monument to America's first citizen. The stark, 555½-foot structure, however, tells us little of Washington the man. It is to Mount Vernon, carefully preserved since 1859 by the Mount Vernon Ladies' Association, that one must return for an appreciation of this most remarkable figure. Today it presents a much greater degree of neatness and prosperity than it probably did 200 years ago, but the orderliness and graceful proportions of the estate and its buildings testify to unerring judgment and good taste. It is here, of course, that Washington was buried. He required no pantheon or mausoleum.

SOME MAXIMS OF WASHINGTON

Think before you speak.

Let your recreations be manful, not sinful.

Speak no evil of the absent, for it is unjust.

Let your conversation be without malice or envy.

Detract not from others, but neither be excessive in commending.

Let your discourse with men of business be short and comprehensive.

Be not apt to relate news if you know not the truth thereof.

Be not hasty to believe flying reports to the disparagement of any one.

Show not yourself glad at the misfortune of another, though he were your enemy.

Undertake not what you cannot perform, but be careful to keep your promise.

Associate yourself with men of good quality if you esteem your reputation.

When a man does all he can, though it succeeds not well, blame not him that
did it.

Labor to keep alive in your breast that little spark of celestial fire called conscience.

WASHINGTON'S CHARACTER

The tributes to Washington's character and greatness would fill many volumes. A few quotations are given below:

Washington the perfect citizen.

R. W. Emerson.

Washington is, to my mind, the purest figure in history.

W. E. Gladstone.

The greatest of good men and the best of great men.

Edward Everett.

In my idea, General Washington is the greatest man, for I look upon him as the most virtuous.

Lafayette.

First in war, first in peace, first in the hearts of his countrymen; he was second to none in the humble and endearing scenes of private life; pious, just, humane, temperate and sincere; uniform, dignified, and commanding, his example was as edifying to all around him as were the effects of that example lasting.

Henry Lee.

Washington's is the mightiest name of earth—long since mightiest in the cause of civil liberty; still mightiest in moral reformation. On that name no eulogy is expected. It cannot be. To add brightness to the sun, or glory to the name of Washington is alike impossible. Let none attempt it. In solemn awe pronounce the name, and in its naked, deathless splendor leave it shining on.

Abraham Lincoln.

THE TWENTY-SECOND
OF FEBRUARY

Pale is the February sky,
  And brief the mid-day's sunny hours;
The wind-swept forest seems to sigh
  For the sweet time of leaves and flowers.

Yet has no month a prouder day,
  Not even when the summer broods
O'er meadows in their fresh array,
  Or autumn tints the glowing woods.

For this chill season now again
  Brings, in its annual round, the morn
When, greatest of the sons of men,
  Our glorious Washington was born.

Lo, where, beneath an icy shield,
  Calmly the mighty Hudson flows!
By snow-clad fell and frozen field,
  Broadening, the lordly river goes.

The wildest storm that sweeps through space,
  And rends the oak with sudden force,
Can raise no ripple on his face,
  Or slacken his majestic course.

Thus, 'mid the wreck of thrones, shall live
  Unmarred, undimmed, our hero's fame,
And years succeeding years shall give
  Increase of honors to his name.

                    William Cullen Bryant

My Greetings to you on Washington's Birthday

WASHINGTON AS A CIVILIAN

However his military fame may excite the wonder of mankind, it is chiefly by his civil magistracy that Washington's example will instruct them. Great generals have arisen in all ages of the world, and perhaps most in those of despotism and darkness. In times of violence and convulsion, they rise, by the force of the whirlwind, high enough to ride in it and direct the storm. Like meteors, they glare on the black clouds with a splendor that, while it dazzles and terrifies, makes nothing visible but the darkness. The fame of heroes is indeed growing vulgar: they multiply in every long war; they stand in history, and thicken in their ranks almost as undistinguished as their own soldiers.

But such a chief magistrate as Washington appears like the pole-star in a clear sky, to direct the skilful statesman. His presidency will form an epoch and be distinguished as the age of Washington. Already it assumes its high place in the political region. Like the milky way, it whitens along its allotted portion of the hemisphere. The latest generations of men will survey, through the telescope of history, the space where so many virtues blend their rays, and delight to separate them into groups and distinct virtues. As the best illustration of them, the living monument to which the first of patriots would have chosen to consign his fame, it is my earnest prayer to heaven that our country may subsist, even to that late date, in the plenitude of its liberty and happiness, and mingle its mild glory with Washington's.

From the Eulogy of Washington, 1800.
Fisher Ames.

WASHINGTON'S PERSONAL APPEARANCE

The following description of Washington's personal appearance is by Theodore Parker:

"In his person Washington was six feet high, and rather slender. His limbs were long, his hands were uncommonly large, his chest broad and full, his head was exactly round, and the hair brown in manhood, but gray at fifty; his forehead rather low and retreating, the nose large and massy, the mouth wide and firm, the chin square and heavy, the cheeks full and ruddy in early life. His eyes blue and handsome, but not quick or nervous. He required spectacles to read with at fifty. He was one of the best riders in the United States, but, like some other good riders, awkward and shambling in his walk. He was stately in his bearing, reserved, distant and apparently haughty. Shy among women he was not a great talker in any company, but a careful observer and listener. He read the natural temper of men, but not always aright. He seldom smiled. Like many grave persons, he was fond of jokes and loved humorous stories. He had negro story tellers to regale him with fun and anecdotes at Mount Vernon. He was not critical about his food, but fond of tea. He took beer or cider at dinner, and occasionally wine. He hated drunkenness, gaming and tobacco. He had a hearty love of farming and of private life. There was nothing of the politician in him, no particle of cunning. He was one of the most industrious of men. Not an elegant or accurate writer, he yet took great pains with his style, and after the Revolution carefully corrected the letters he had written in the time of the French War, more than thirty years before. He was no orator, like Jefferson, Franklin, Madison and others, who had great influence in American affairs."

Eng. by A.B. Durand from the full length Portrait by Col. Trumbull belonging to Yale College.

GEORGE WASHINGTON.

MOUNT VERNON

There dwelt the Man, the flower of human-kind,
　　Whose visage mild bespoke his nobler mind.

There dwelt the Soldier, who his sword ne'er drew
　　But in a righteous cause, to Freedom true.

There dwelt the Hero, who ne'er killed for fame,
　　Yet gained more glory than a Cæsar's name.

There dwelt the Statesman, who, devoid of art,
　　Gave soundest counsels from an upright heart;

And O Columbia, by thy sons caressed,
　　There dwelt the Father of the realms he blessed;

Who no wish felt to make his mighty praise,
　　Like other chiefs, the means himself to raise;

But there retiring, breathed in pure renown,
　　And felt a grandeur that disdained a crown.

William Day

THREE OLD TALES
BY PARSON WEEMS

I. THE CHERRY TREE

When George was about six years old, he was made the wealthy master of a hatchet of which, like most little boys, he was extremely fond. He went about chopping everything that came his way.

One day, as he wandered about the garden amusing himself by hacking his mother's peasticks, he found a beautiful, young English cherry tree, of which his father was most proud. He tried the edge of his hatchet on the trunk of the tree and barked it so that it died.

Some time after this, his father discovered what had happened to his favorite tree. He came into the house in great anger, and demanded to know who the mischievous person was who had cut away the bark. Nobody could tell him anything about it.

Just then George, with his little hatchet, came into the room.

"George," said his father, "do you know who has killed my beautiful little cherry tree yonder in the garden? I would not have taken five guineas for it!"

This was a hard question to answer, and for a moment George was staggered by it, but quickly recovering himself he cried:—

"I cannot tell a lie, father, you know I cannot tell a lie! I did cut it with my little hatchet."

The anger died out of his father's face, and taking the boy tenderly in his arms, he said:—

"My son, that you should not be afraid to tell the truth is more to me than a thousand trees! yes, though they were blossomed with silver and had leaves of the purest gold!"

II. THE APPLE ORCHARD

One fine morning in the autumn, Mr. Washington, taking little George by the hand, walked with him to the apple orchard, promising that he would show him a fine sight.

On arriving at the orchard they saw a fine sight, indeed! The green grass under the trees was strewn with red-cheeked apples, and yet the trees were bending under the weight of fruit that hung thick among the leaves.

"Now, George," said his father, "look my son, see all this rich harvest of fruit! Do you remember when your good cousin brought you a fine, large apple last spring, how you refused to divide it with your brothers? And yet I told you then that, if you would be generous, God would give you plenty of apples this autumn."

Poor George could not answer, but hanging down his head looked quite confused, while with his little, naked, bare feet he scratched in the soft ground.

"Now, look up, my son," continued his father, "and see how the blessed God has richly

provided us with these trees loaded with the finest fruit. See how abundant is the harvest. Some of the trees are bending beneath their burdens, while the ground is covered with mellow apples, more than you could eat, my son, in all your lifetime."

George looked in silence on the orchard, he marked the busy, humming bees, and heard the gay notes of the birds fluttering from tree to tree. His eyes filled with tears and he answered softly:—

"Truly, father, I never will be selfish any more."

III. THE GARDEN-BED

One day Mr. Washington went into the garden and dug a little bed of earth and prepared it for seed. He then took a stick and traced on the bed George's name in full. After this he strewed the tracing thickly with seeds, and smoothed all over nicely with his roller.

This garden-bed he purposely prepared close to a gooseberry-walk. The bushes were hung with the ripe fruit, and he knew that George would visit them every morning.

Not many days had passed away when one morning George came running into the house, breathless with excitement, and his eyes shining with happiness.

"Come here! father, come here!" he cried.

"What's the matter, my son?" asked his father.

"O come, father," answered George, "and I'll show you such a sight as you have never seen in all your lifetime."

Mr. Washington gave the boy his hand, which he seized with great eagerness. He led his father straight to the garden-bed, whereon in large letters, in lines of soft green, was written:— GEORGE WASHINGTON

LIKE WASHINGTON

We cannot all be Washingtons,
  And have our birthdays celebrated;
But we can love the things he loved,
  And we can hate the things he hated.

He loved the truth, he hated lies,
  He minded what his mother taught him,
And every day he tried to do
  The simple duties that it brought him.

Perhaps the reason little folks
  Are sometimes great when they grow taller,
Is just because, like Washington,
  They do their best when they are smaller.

Unknown

WASHINGTON'S COMMON-SENSE

Common sense was eminently a characteristic of Washington; so called, not because it is so very common a trait of character of public men, but because it is the final judgment on great practical questions to which the mind of the community is pretty sure eventually to arrive. Few qualities of character in those who influence the fortunes of nations are so conducive both to stability and progress. But it is a quality which takes no hold of the imagination; it inspires no enthusiasm; it wins no favor; it is well if it can stand its ground against the plausible absurdities, the hollow pretenses, the stupendous impostures of the day.

I believe, as I do in my existence, that it was an important part in the design of Providence in raising Washington up to be a leader of the Revolutionary struggle, and afterwards the first President of the United States, to rebuke prosperous ambition and successful intrigue; to set before the people of America, in the morning of their national existence, a living example to prove that armies may be best conducted, and governments most ably and honorably administered, by men of sound moral principle; to teach to gifted and aspiring individuals and the parties they lead, that, though a hundred crooked paths may conduct to a temporary success, the one plain and straight path of public and private virtue can alone lead to a pure and lasting fame and the blessings of posterity.

Edward Everett.

WASHINGTON

Where may the wearied eye repose
   When gazing on the great;
Where neither guilty glory glows,
   Nor despicable state?
Yes—one—the first—the last—the best—
The Cincinnatus of the West,
   Whom envy dared not hate,
Bequeathed the name of Washington,
To make man blush there was but one!

George Gordon Byron

AT THE TOMB OF WASHINGTON

Here let the brows be bared
　　Before the land's great son,
He who undaunted dared,
　　Our Washington!

From dole, despair and doubt,
　　Deceit and enmity,
He led us up and out
　　To Victory.

A Pharos in the night,
　　A pillar in the dawn,
By his inspiring light
　　May we fare on!

Day upon hastening day
　　Still let us reverence him;
Fame never, never may
　　His laurels dim!

Clinton Scollard

St. Patrick's Day

It is impossible to say when the 17th of March was first set apart as St. Patrick's Day and observed as the popular holiday of Ireland, but it is now celebrated throughout Ireland as a national holiday, and the festival is observed by Irishmen everywhere. In most of the cities of America it is celebrated by various Irish organizations and by other citizens of Irish blood by parades, speeches, and banquets—not to mention general good-natured carousing, feasts of corned-beef and cabbage, and liberal helpings of good Irish whiskey enjoyed not only by Irishmen, but by all who admire the Emerald Isle. In Ireland itself, the celebration is less formal, but it is more universal. The shamrock is worn by everyone, in commemoration of the fact that when St. Patrick was preaching the doctrine of the Trinity he made use of the plant bearing three leaves upon one stem as a symbol of the Holy Trinity. (The earliest celebration of St. Patrick's Day in America is treated elsewhere in this chapter.)

St. Patrick, the patron saint and apostle of Ireland, is one of the most celebrated of the early Christian saints. There is much doubt and uncertainty regarding the events and dates in St. Patrick's life, and particularly as to the place and date of his birth. This is especially strange as he left an account of his life in what is known as his *Confession,* but this work gives few details of dates and events, being principally devoted to his missionary labors. In this document he says he was born at "Banavem Taberniae." The best authorities now agree that this was a village in the Roman province of Britain on the river Clyde, and probably identical with the present town of Dumbarton, a few miles northwest of Glasgow, Scotland. The date of his birth varies greatly with different authorities, but was probably about the year 387.

His parents were Christians. His father's name was Calphurnius and his mother was named Conchessa. His father was evidently a man of means and standing, as he was a deacon of the church and also a *decurion,* that is, one of the council or magistracy of a Roman town. St. Patrick's baptismal name was Succat. Until he was sixteen years old he lived the usual life of a farmer's son of his time. When he was sixteen years of age, he was captured by pirates and carried to Ireland, where he was sold as a slave to Milchu, a Celtic chieftain in the county of Antrim. Here he lived as a slave for six years and was employed in tending cattle.

Near the end of the sixth year of his captivity, he dreamed that he was soon to return to his parents and that on the seacoast he would find a ship that would carry him home. After escaping, he journeyed south for about 200 miles and, when he reached the coast, found a ship ready to sail. After being at first refused, he was finally taken on board as a servant and, after a voyage of three days, reached land. He does not state what land it was, but some writers say it was France. Wherever it may have been, he had to travel for twenty-eight days through a wild desert country before he reached a civilized place. After further journeys and many hardships, he finally reached home.

During his captivity he had learned the Gaelic language, and after his escape a vision summoned him to return to Ireland as a missionary. According to some authorities, before returning to Ireland he traveled in France and Italy and received his apostolic benediction from Pope Celestine in the year 432. It was on the occasion of his consecration that he assumed the name of Patrick, by which name he is now exclusively known. In his *Confession,* St. Patrick does not state when or where he was consecrated as bishop, but it is certain that he exercised the powers and functions of that office and his authority to do so was never doubted.

He began his missionary work in Ireland about the year 433 and the rest of his life was spent in incessant labors which were amply rewarded. When he came to Ireland there were no Christians there and when he died there were no heathens! The common people received the new faith with great readiness, but he met with much opposition from the Druid priests and the ruling Celtic classes, and St. Patrick and the early converts suffered much persecution from them. The magnitude of his work in Ireland may be appreciated when it is said that he founded 385 churches and placed a school by the side of each; he organized at least one archiepiscopal see, that of Armagh; consecrated a number of bishops; established one or two colleges; and civilized the people generally.

Many miracles are attributed to St. Patrick. One of the best known is his driving the snakes out of Ireland. Another legend tells how he made a fire out of ice and snow balls. There are also many accounts of his miraculous escapes from his enemies.

St. Patrick preached in Ireland for about thirty years. The date of his death has been much disputed. According to the best authorities, he died on the 17th of March in the year 463, though others say 493. He was buried at Downpatrick, in the province of Ulster, about twenty-one miles southeast of Belfast.

St. Patrick is said to have been a man of small stature, but of great energy and activity of mind and body, and we have some proof that his very aspect must have inspired regard and respect. He was truly humble, wore coarse garments, and worked cheerfully and diligently with his own hands. He was, according to one early commentator, "most sweet and affable in conversation, by which he accommodated himself to all sorts and conditions of people, and did so gain their affections that if it could be done, they would have plucked out their eyes and given them to him." Countless gifts were pressed upon him, which he always refused unless they were meant to relieve the poor or to build religious houses. He slept on the bare ground, a stone for his pillow, until he was fifty-five years old.

Is it any wonder that this exemplar of strength and dignity should so inspire a nation so long torn by strife—or that so many sons of Ireland in America should continue to venerate St. Patrick and the wearing of the green?

SAINT PATRICKS DAY.

ST. PATRICK'S DAY IN AMERICA

According to John D. Crimmins, in his work entitled "St. Patrick's Day," the earliest recorded observance of the day in America occurred in 1737. On March 17th of that year a number of the leading Irish Protestants of Boston celebrated the occasion by organizing the Charitable Irish Society. This society is still in existence, though now there is no religious qualification for membership.

Several celebrations of St. Patrick's Day are recorded during the French and Indian Wars. On March 17, 1757, a celebration took place at Fort William Henry, on Lake George, which had a large number of Irishmen in its garrison. On the evening of the 17th, the French army having made a forced march from Ticonderoga, attacked Fort William Henry thinking to find the garrison unprepared because of the festival. But in this they were disappointed and they were repulsed with considerable loss. In 1763, St. Patrick's Day was celebrated at Fort Pitt, now Pittsburg.

St. Patrick's Day was observed by both the American and British armies during the Revolution on several occasions. The British evacuated Boston and the Americans marched in and took possession on March 17, 1776. Washington authorized as the pass-word for the day "Boston" and the countersign "St. Patrick." In Philadelphia in 1778, St. Patrick's Day was celebrated by men in the British forces. A contemporary writes: "A crowd of Irish soldiers went by this afternoon, with one on horseback representing St. Patrick." There was also an observance of the festival by the American army at Valley Forge in 1778. On this occasion there was considerable trouble because of the pranks which some of the soldiers played at the expense of their Irish comrades. The Irishmen were greatly incensed and quite a disturbance ensued. Washington appeared personally and after giving them a kindly lecture promised to punish those who had given offense to the Irishmen. Then, the chronicler says, "there was an extra issue of grog to the army and thus all made merry and were good friends." When the Americans were stationed at Morristown, New Jersey, in 1780, Washington issued an order authorizing the celebration of St. Patrick's Day.

There are also records of other early celebrations of the festival in New York, Philadelphia, Boston, and other places throughout the country. These scattered, and occasional celebrations became more regular and wide spread as the Irish population increased. By the middle of the nineteenth century the observance of St. Patrick's Day had become a fixed custom in the principal American cities and now the anniversary is observed in almost every city and town in the country.

Anonymous, 1913

THE BIRTH
OF ST. PATRICK

On the eighth day of March it was, some people say,
That Saint Pathrick at midnight he first saw the day;
While others declare 'twas the ninth he was born,
And 'twas all a mistake, between midnight and morn;
For mistakes will occur in a hurry and shock,
And some blamed the babby—and some blamed the clock—
Till with all their cross-questions sure no one could know
If the child was too fast, or the clock was too slow.

Now the first faction-fight in ould Ireland, they say,
Was all on account of St. Pathrick's birthday;
Some fought for the eighth—for the ninth more would die,
And who wouldn't see right, sure they blacken'd his eye!
At last, both the factions so positive grew,
That each kept a birthday, so Pat then had two,
Till Father Mulcahy, who show'd them their sins,
Said, "No one could have two birthdays, but a twins."

Says he, "Boys, don't be fightin' for eight or for nine,
Don't be always dividin'—but sometimes combine;
Combine eight with nine, and seventeen is the mark,
So let that be his birthday,"—"Amen," says the clerk.
"If he wasn't a twins, sure our hist'ry will show
That, at least, he's worth any two saints that we know!"
Then they all got blind dhrunk—which complated their bliss,
And we keep up the practice from that day to this.

Samuel Lover

THE GREEN LITTLE SHAMROCK
OF IRELAND

There's a dear little plant that grows in our isle,
    Twas St. Patrick himself, sure, that set it;
And the sun on his labor with pleasure did smile,
    And with dew from his eye often wet it.
It thrives through the bog,
        through the brake,
        through the mireland.
And he called it the dear little shamrock of Ireland.
        The sweet little shamrock, the dear little shamrock,
        The sweet little, green little shamrock of Ireland.

This dear little plant that springs from our soil,
    When its three little leaves are extended,
Denotes on one stalk we together should toil,
    And ourselves by ourselves be befriended;
And still through the bog,
        through the brake,
        through the mireland,
From one root should branch, like the shamrock of Ireland.
        The sweet little shamrock, the dear little shamrock,
        The sweet little, green little shamrock of Ireland!

Andrew Cherry

NEW YORK CITY.—MAYOR WICKHAM REVIEWING, IN FRONT OF THE CITY HALL, THE PROCESSION IN HONOR OF THE IRISH NATIONAL HOLIDAY, ST. PATRICK'S DAY, MARCH 17TH.—SEE PAGE 54.

THE WEARIN' O' THE GREEN

O Paddy dear! an' did ye hear the news that's goin' round?
The shamrock is by law forbid to grow on Irish ground!
No more St. Patrick's day we'll keep, his color can't be seen,
For there's a cruel law agin the wearin' o' the green!
I met wid Napper Tandy, and he took me by the hand,
And he said, "How's poor Ould Ireland, and how does she stand?"
She's the most disthressful country that iver yet was seen,
For they're hangin' men and women there for wearin' o' the green.

An' if the color we must wear is England's cruel red,
Let it remind us of the blood that Ireland has shed;
Then pull the shamrock from your hat, and throw it on the sod,—
And never fear, 'twill take root there, tho' under foot 'tis trod!
When law can stop the blades of grass from growin' as they grow,
And when the leaves in summer-time their color dare not show,
Then will I change the color, too, I wear in my caubeen,
But till that day, plaze God, I'll stick to wearin' o' the green.

Unknown

All Fools' Day (April Fools' Day)

"Many explanations have been offered for the custom of playing practical jokes on the first of April," writes George William Douglas in his superb, but long out-of-print *American Book of Days,* "but there is agreement on one of them. The impression prevails, however, that the custom has something to do with the observance of the spring equinox. In India the Feast of Huli, which occurs on March 31, has been celebrated for numberless centuries by sending people on foolish errands. One fantastic explanation is that the custom arose from a farcical celebration of the sending of Jesus from Annas to Caiphus, from Caiphus to Pilate, from Pilate to Herod, and from Herod back to Pilate at the time of the trial and crucifixion. But this is not taken seriously. Another theory is that it is a relic of the Roman Cerealia, held at the beginning of April. According to the legend, Proserpina had filled her lap with daffodils in the Elysian meadows when Pluto found her and carried her screaming to the lower world. Ceres, her mother, heard the echo of the screams and went in search of the voice, but her search was like a fool's errand for it was impossible to find the echo.

"April fooling became customary in France after the adoption of the reformed calendar by Charles IX in 1564, making the year begin on January 1. It had previously been common for the people to make new year's gifts and exchange calls on April 1 under the old calendar, and conservatives objected to the change. Wags accordingly sent to these persons mock gifts on April 1 and made calls of pretended ceremony. Nowadays the person fooled in France is called a *poisson d'avril,* that is, an April fish. Whether this is because the sun is leaving the zodiacal sign of Pisces at the time or because April fish are easily caught, no one knows. It was not until the beginning of the eighteenth century that April fooling became common in England. In Scotland the April fools are called April gowks, the gowk being a cuckoo. The early settlers in America brought the custom with them. It is observed here chiefly by small boys. They will write 'Kick Me' on a piece of paper and pin it surreptitiously on the back of a companion, and await the result with ill-suppressed glee. They will also pin a card with April Fool written on another's coat. They will tie a string to a purse, drop the purse on the sidewalk and then conceal themselves with the end of the string in their hands. When some one stoops to pick up the purse, they pull it out of his reach. Sometimes they nail a purse to a board and fool the unsuspecting. Or they put a brick under an old hat and wait for some one to try to kick it out of his way. Balls of cotton covered with chocolate to look like candies are also prepared as well as balls of pepper and salt. Little children find delight in telling one of their elders that there is a hole in his sock or a thread on his coat or a black spot on his cheek and then laughing uproariously as the victim looks for it, and shouting April Fool!

"Their elders are not immune to the temptation to play practical jokes on the day. It has been common in cities in which there is an aquarium or a zoological garden for a man to tell another in his office to call up such and such a telephone number, giving the number of the aquarium or the zoo, as Mr. Fish or Mr. Camel wished to speak to him. The custom became so annoying to those in charge of the Aquarium and the Zoological Garden in New York that they have had their telephones disconnected on April 1. In towns without such natural history collections, the butcher's telephone number is given to the victim and he is told that Mr. Lamb has a message for him."

George William Douglas wrote the preceding words more than forty years ago. That little has changed in the intervening years is obvious. That little has changed in more than a century may be seen from a passage written in 1877 that appears elsewhere in this section. And that little has changed in the celebration of April Fool's Day over the centuries is evident in the following passage from *The Looker-On,* an English work published almost 200 years ago:

"1st April, 1790—Got up early this morning, to prepare for business—Sally still a-bed—Flung the watchman a shilling out of the window, to rap at my door, and cry fire—Sally started up in a fright, overturned my best wig, which stood in the passage, and ran into the street half dressed. Was obliged to give her a shilling to quiet her.

"Ten o'clock.—Sent a letter to Mr. Plume, the undertaker, telling him that my neighbor old Frank Fuz, who was married on Monday to his late wife's step-daughter, had died suddenly last night—Saw six of Plume's men go in, and heard old Fuz very loud with them.

"Invited all our club to dine at deputy Dripping's, and invited him to dine with alderman Grub, at Hampstead—(The alderman is actually on a visit to his son-in-law in Kent.)

"One o'clock—Afraid Sally would play some trick on me in dressing my dinner; so went to get a steak at a coffee-house. Chalked the waiter's back as he gave me my change.—(On leaving, noticed that the waiter had given *me* two bad shillings!)

"Asked an old woman in Cheapside what was the matter with her hat?—She took it off; and while I was calling her April fool, a boy ran off with my handkerchief in his hand.

"Tapped a Blue-school boy on the shoulder, and asked what he had got behind him? He answered, a fool—The people laughed at this. *I* did not see much in it.

"Gave Giles, my shopman, a glass of brandy, which he took for a glass of wine. Giles unable to attend shop the next day."

As should be obvious by now, *plus ça change, plus c'est la même chose.* The more things change, the more they remain the same—especially among practical jokers.

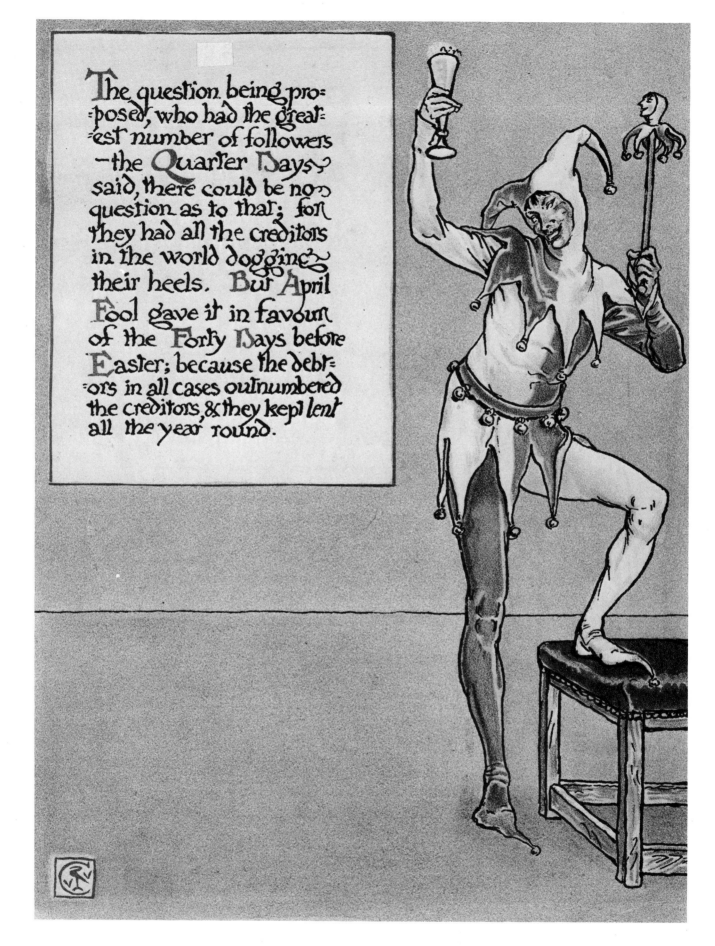

The question being pro=posed, who had the great=est number of followers —the Quarter Days, said, there could be no question as to that; for they had all the creditors in the world dogging their heels. But April Fool gave it in favour of the Forty Days before Easter; because the debt=ors in all cases outnumbered the creditors, & they kept lent all the year round.

FOURTH MONTH DUNCE

The curious custom of joking on the first of April, sending the ignorant or the unwary on fruitless errands, for the sake of making them feel foolish and having a laugh at them, prevails very widely in the world. And whether you call the victim a "Fourth month dunce," an "April fool," an "April fish" (as in France), or an "April gowk" (as in Scotland), the object, to deceive him and laugh at him, is everywhere the same.

The custom has been traced back for ages; all through Europe, as far back as the records go. The "Feast of Fools" is mentioned as celebrated by the ancient Romans. In Asia the Hindoos have a festival, ending on the 31st of March, called the "Huli festival," in which they play the same sort of first of April pranks—translated into Hindoo—laughing at the victim, and making him a "Huli fool." It goes back even to Persia, where it is supposed to have a beginning, in very ancient times in the celebration of spring, when their New Year begins.

How it came to be what we everywhere find it, the wise men cannot agree. The many authorities are so divided that I see no way but for us to accept the custom as we find it, wherever we may happen to be, and be careful not to abuse it.

Some jokes are peculiar to particular places. In England, where it is called All Fools' Day, one favorite joke is to send the greenhorn to a bookseller to buy the "Life and Adventures of Eve's Grandmother," or to a cobbler to buy a few cents' worth of "strap oil,"—strap oil being, in the language of the shoemaking brotherhood, a personal application of the leather. The victim usually gets a good whipping with a strap.

In Scotland the first of April fun is called "hunting the gowk," and consists most often of sending a person to another a long way off, with a note which says, "Hunt the gowk another mile." The recipient of the note gives him a new missive to still another, containing the same words; and so the sport goes on, till the victim remembers the day of the month, and sits down to rest and think about it.

In France, where the custom is very ancient, the jokes are much the same; but the victim is called an "April fish," because he is easily caught. In one part of France there is a custom of eating a certain kind of peas which grow there, called *pois chiches.* The joke there is to send the peasants to a certain convent to ask for those peas, telling them that the fathers are obliged to give some to every one who comes on that day. The joke is as much on the monks as on the peasants, for there is often a perfect rush of applicants all day.

I need not tell you the American styles of joking—nailing a piece of silver to the side-walk; tying a string to a purse, and jerking it away from greedy fingers; leaving tempting-looking packages, filled with sand, on door-steps; frying doughnuts with an interlining of wool; putting salt in the sugar bowl, etc. You know too many already.

But this custom, with others, common in coarser and rougher times, is fast dying out. Even now it is left almost entirely to playful children. This sentiment, quoted from an English almanac of a hundred years ago, will, I'm sure, meet the approval of "grown-ups" of the nineteenth century:

But 'tis a thing to be disputed,
Which is the greatest fool reputed,
The one that innocently went,
Or he that him designedly sent.

Anonymous, 1877

APRIL FOOL LAND

There's a joyful land, I understand,
　　For the folks who know the way;
It's hard to learn the place to turn,
　　And it can't be reached in a day.
　　　　Oh, a tricksy road
　　　　And a mixey road,
　　That leads to the Joyful Town,
Where every rule is April Fool
　　And streets run upside down.

Policemen bold are clowns, I'm told,
　　And all the money is jokes.
And as for the King, in the land I sing,
　　He's the fellow that's best at a hoax.
　　　　Oh, the royal crown
　　　　In the Joyful Town
　　Is the jingling Jester's cap,
For every rule is April Fool
　　And every door a trap!

With wily care must you beware
　　Of the sign-posts in that town;
They always sound the other way round,
　　And they're mostly upside down.
　　　　The pie-crusts hide
　　　　White mice inside,
　　And the frightened guests all scream—
For every rule is April Fool
　　And school's an idle dream.

Small children play their tricks all day,
　　And never are spanked at all;
And harlequins with pointed chins
　　Are gleefully playing ball.
　　　　The rain and sun
　　　　Join in the fun
　　To trick the Weather Man—
For every rule is April Fool
　　And cooks play Patty-Pan!

Now, once a year the folk come here,
　　And a joyful time have they!

They turn the town quite upside down
　　On April Fool—his day.
　　　　If I could find
　　　　The roads that wind
　　Across to Joyful Town,
I'd backward run and have some fun
　　With Harlequin and Clown,
Where every rule is April Fool
　　And streets lead upside down!

George Phillips

AN APRIL FOOL

When Uncle Robert got his mail
  That First-of-April morning
(Now, absent-minded people all,
  Just read and take a warning),

Among the business bills and slips,
  And cards of invitation,
And friendly notes, he found, at last,
  One queer communication.

It took but little time to read—
  A moment but to con it:

The two words "April Fool!" were all
  That could be found upon it.

Then Uncle Robert laughed and said:
  "I've heard of funny blunders
In superscription and address,
  And many puzzling wonders,

"And seen epistles left unsigned.
  This goes them all one better:
For here's a man who signed his name
  And forgot to write the letter!"

Abby F.C. Bates

Arbor Day

In no country in the Western world is a day set aside for the priase and planting of trees more to be desired. Arbor Day—first celebrated in Nebraska in 1872—is such a festival, but one celebrated officially in only that prairie state and in Utah. Unofficial observances are held in various other states during the months from February through May. In some schools throughout the country, Arbor Day—usually April 22nd—is observed by the planting of a tree by students. The practice, however, has been on the wane in recent years, a curious trend in light of current interest in environmental conditions and in the enjoyment of nature. At a time when there has been a considerable loss of greenery in our towns and countryside due to an influx of new varieties of predatory insects and a marked increase in man's ability to pave over the earth, Arbor Day is a most relevant, useful exercise in civic responsibility.

The need for such an observance was first recognized by J. Sterling Morton in the late 1860s. A settler in the Nebraska Territory, he understood the benefits which would be enjoyed by the planting of trees on the prairie then being cut up into farmland—as windbreaks, fuel, lumber, and shade. Hundreds of miles of fertile land was being brought into useful cultivation, land that had once stood as a vast sea of grasses. Early ecologists such as Morton understood the necessity of replacing one form of natural growth with another while still providing for the pursuit of agriculture. Many rural areas to the east and the south had already been badly disfigured and despoiled by the indiscriminate removal of natural and useful beauty in the form of trees. And these were areas in which—unlike the prairie lands—trees were a natural part of the landscape. Writers in almost all of the major nineteenth-century agricultural magazines urged farmers to provide shade for their houses, rows of trees in the fields to prevent erosion and encourage the flow of natural springs, woodlots which could yield an almost endless supply of fuel if carefully cut and replanted, and attractive plantings along the roadsides. This advice was followed only to a minor degree.

The results of the misuse of the land—especially the removal of trees—became abundantly evident by the early twentieth century. Conservationists such as Theodore Roosevelt and John Muir acted to save as much of the Far West's forests and streams as was possible. The redwoods of California stood as a particularly graphic symbol of the need to preserve the past for the future. National parks were established in all areas of the country, and cities and towns which had grown haphazardly during most of the nineteenth century, stopped to plan pleasant parks and promenades. Children did plant trees in schoolyards and before other civic structures. But not enough was done. In the Depression years of the 1930s the wanton use of farmland was laid bare by drought and pestilence for all to see. And by the 1950s, even the city dweller could view the devastating results of ever-widening roads, sprawling housing developments, and industrial pollution. America the beautiful it was no longer.

Morton's dream—and that of scores of men and women before and after—was that America could be as verdant and as productive a land as those of the Old World. This meant planning and planting for the future. Of Arbor Day, he wrote:

Other Holidays Repose upon the Past—
Arbor Day Proposes for the Future.

So it is. Most other holidays celebrate an event in history. Arbor Day means an investment in a better tomorrow. It is a quiet, thoughtful day, and the results of the celebration are realized slowly, sometimes only generations later.

Fortunately, some of our ancestors took time to make this investment in the future. Giant oaks still stand in scattered areas of the country; redwoods have been protected; even the magnificent American elm—under severe attack from Dutch elm disease—is carefully tended in many communities. 4-H groups, county agricultural societies, environmental societies such as the Sierra Club, Friends of the Earth, and the Nature Conservancy do their best to see that we do not lose sight of our natural heritage. With fossil fuels escalating in cost, the practical use of wood for energy has even brought back the principles of careful woodlot management to the homestead in rural areas. Why not then celebrate Arbor Day, as was the practice in the late nineteenth and early twentieth centuries?

Arbor Day should not be, however, a day only for children. Other countries have followed the American practice of setting aside a special time for planting trees. In such a new land as Israel, the planting of whole forests has been a necessity; memorials to loved ones in the form of groves of fruit and shade trees has immeasurably enriched whole areas. John Chapman, the Johnny Appleseed of legend, spread the doctrine of apple growing from New York to Indiana in the first half of the nineteenth century. America has other popular heroes from the past who have similarly enriched the lives of all of us—Luther Burbank, Birdsey G. Northrup, Henry David Thoreau, John Muir, John Burroughs, George Washington Carver, Theodore Roosevelt—by preaching the good word of conservation. The word "arbor" is taken from the Latin for "tree" and can have as much meaning in the New World as it has had in the Old.

PLANT TREES

Plant trees and care for them. They will repay you for many years to come in fruit and nuts and flowers; and will afford protection for man, beast, and bird against the piercing rays of old Sol in summer, and the fierce blasts of rude Boreas in winter. Plant trees.

Anonymous

AN ARBOR DAY TREE

Dear little tree that we plant to-day,
What will you be when we're old and gray?
   "The savings bank of the squirrel and mouse,
   For robin and wren an apartment house,
The dressing-room of the butterfly's ball,
The locust's and katydid's concert hall,
   The schoolboy's ladder in pleasant June,
   The schoolgirl's tent in the July noon,
And my leaves shall whisper them merrily
A tale of the children who planted me."

Anonymous

TREES

I think that I shall never see
A poem lovely as a tree.

A tree whose hungry mouth is pressed
Against the earth's sweet flowing breast;

A tree that looks at God all day
And lifts her leafy arms to pray;

A tree that may in summer wear
A nest of robins in her hair;

Upon whose bosom snow has lain;
Who intimately lives with rain.

Poems are made by fools like me,
But only God can make a tree.

Joyce Kilmer

WHAT DO WE PLANT?

What do we plant when we plant the tree?
We plant the ship which will cross the sea,
We plant the mast to carry the sails,
We plant the planks to withstand the gales—
The keel, the keelson, and beam and knee,—
We plant the ship when we plant the tree.

What do we plant when we plant the tree?
We plant the houses for you and me.
We plant the rafters, the shingles, the floors,
We plant the studding, the lath, the doors,
The beams and siding, all parts that be,
We plant the house when we plant the tree.

What do we plant when we plant the tree?
A thousand things that we daily see.
We plant the spire that out-towers the crag,
We plant the staff for our country's flag,
We plant the shade from the hot sun free;
We plant all these when we plant the tree.

Henry Abbey

WHEN WE PLANT A TREE

When we plant a tree, we are doing what we can to make our planet a more wholesome and happier dwelling-place for those who come after us, if not for ourselves. As you drop the seed, as you plant the sapling, your left hand hardly knows what your right hand is doing. But Nature knows, and in due time the Power that sees and works in secret will reward you openly. You have been warned against hiding your talent in a napkin; but if your talent takes the form of a maple-key or an acorn, and your napkin is a shred of the apron that covers "the lap of the earth," you may hide it there, unblamed; and when you render in your account you will find that your deposit has been drawing compound interest all the time.

Oliver Wendell Holmes.

THE FOREST

Who shall describe the inexpressible tenderness and immortal life of the grim forest, where Nature, though it be mid-winter, is ever in her spring, where the moss-grown and decaying trees are not old, but seem to enjoy a perpetual youth; and blissful, innocent nature, like a serene infant, is too happy to make a noise, except by a few tinkling, lisping birds and trickling rills?

Henry D. Thoreau.

HE WHO PLANTS AN OAK

He who plants an oak looks forward to future ages, and plants for posterity. Nothing can be less selfish than this. He cannot expect to sit in its shade nor enjoy its shelter; but he exults in the idea that the acorn which he has buried in the earth shall grow up into a lofty pile, and shall keep on flourishing and increasing, and benefiting mankind, long after he shall have ceased to tread his paternal fields. The oak, in the pride and lustihood of its growth, seems to me to take its range with the lion and the eagle, and to assimilate, in the grandeur of its attributes, to heroic and intellectual man.

With its mighty pillar rising straight and direct toward heaven, bearing up its leafy honors from the impurities of earth, and supporting them aloft in free air and glorious sunshine, it is an emblem of what a true nobleman should be; a refuge for the weak—a shelter for the oppressed—a defense for the defenseless; warding off from them the peltings of the storm, or the scorching rays of arbitrary power.

Washington Irving.

Pl. 298.

Chêne à fruits pédonculés. Quercus pedonculata Ehrh.

Easter

Easter has always meant a new beginning. It is celebrated each year just as Spring arrives on the scene, bringing with it the signs of awakening from a long winter—tender green foliage, the first flowers of a new year, the return of fair weather birds from southern climes. Because the date varies from year to year, celebrants of this most Christian of festivals may find themselves on their way to church through receding snow drifts or along mud-caked roads. Still, even in the coldest reaches of North America, some sense of the renewal of life can be felt in the lengthening hours of daylight and the swelling of the branches in trees and shrubs. Since 325 A.D., observance of the holiday has been set as the first Sunday following the first full moon after the vernal equinox, March 21st. This was a decision of the Council of Nicaea and has never been followed by Eastern Christians who require that Easter also follow the Jewish Passover. People of the Orthodox faith throughout the world thus celebrate the holiday somewhat later than Western Christians.

Like other essentially religious festival days, Easter has been greatly secularized. Although it remains a sacred event for Christians celebrating the resurrection of Christ from the tomb and the promise of eternal life, the day may be one for the display of new finery, a welcome opportunity for a family outing, or even an excuse for young people to perform the rites of Spring in warm vacation spots. All of these practices—"pagan" in spirit—only point out the natural yearning of people to welcome the return of the sun. In so doing, they are carrying on traditions which have been recorded since the most ancient of times.

The early Protestant settlers of New England frowned on even the most spiritual of Easter rites. Their influence, however, was to be dissipated by the combined emigration of middle-European Protestants and Roman Catholics from the mid-eighteenth to the late nineteenth centuries. German settlers, who so shaped the celebration of Christmas in America, were also responsible for introducing many of the Easter customs which are enjoyed today. The word "Easter" is derived from the old Saxon name for the goddess of spring, "Eostre." Her festival was celebrated at the time of the vernal equinox. And before the Gregorian calendar was introduced in 1582, the festival of "Eostre" was akin to that of New Year's. Just as Christians today celebrate a new beginning in Christ on Easter Sunday, the worshippers of the gods and goddesses danced to the first full moon of the new year and to the rising of the sun.

The hare, rather than the rabbit, was the animal of ancient times associated with Eostre. Born with eyes open, rather than closed like the rabbit, it has been a symbol of the full moon. It is the rabbit, somehow, that has survived as a modern symbol of Easter. Almost as ancient an icon of early renewal is the simple egg. Eggs have been decorated for many hundreds of years by both Christians and earlier believers in a divine source of life. The plastic supermarket eggs of today are, of course, only dull copies of the splendidly ornate creations of Latin and Eastern Orthodox Christians. Painted brilliant colors and decorated with fine materials—sometimes even precious stones—they were gifts to be treasured.

The Easter bunny has been bringing candy and brightly colored eggs to American children of all faiths for generations. This friendly creature was first introduced to the American scene in the nineteenth century by German immigrants. Today he may be found hiding eggs to be discovered on Easter morn at home or perched in a department store nest in the guise of "Egbert," or "Uncle Wiggly," or "Peter Rabbit." Children are invited to have their pictures taken with the friendly cottontail. A less harmless modern tradition has been the giving of baby chicks to children on Easter Sunday. This practice, fortunately, has been on the wane recently, thanks to the attention of animal lovers.

In the 1880s yet another symbol of Eastertide was introduced—the Easter lily. The altar or chancel area of a Christian church is often banked in a profusion of such blooms. This flower, a Bermuda or white trumpet lily, was brought from the Atlantic island to Philadelphia by Mrs. Thomas P. Sargent. The fragrance is sweet and redolent with the promise of spring.

The joyful character of Easter is the festival's most attractive feature. For the Christian who proclaims the message, "Christ the Lord is Risen; He is Risen indeed!", the past is forgotten. The death and passion of Christ is celebrated with new-found strength. Although those departed from the earth are remembered in prayers and thoughts, it is the promise of eternal life—as symbolized in the return of Spring—which is cherished anew. The fervor felt by many of the faithful is only deepened by forty days of fasting in Lent preceding Easter Sunday, and in the rites of Holy Week.

In so abstaining from meat or other desired foods or practices, the Christian is following knowingly or not, one of the most ancient of religious traditions. Members of non-Christian faiths have prepared for sacred occasions through fasting, denying their physical needs, since almost the beginning of recorded history. The faith of all people—however secular it may appear in expression and form—is tested and heightened by denial. It is thereby rendered more truly joyful and comforting. Winter shall return again, but so shall Spring and with it—another Easter.

THE EASTER BUNNY

There's a story quite funny,
About a toy bunny,
And the wonderful things she can do;
Every bright Easter morning,
Without any warning,
She colors eggs, red, green, or blue.

Some she covers with spots,
Some with quaint little dots,
And some with strange mixed colors, too—
Red and green, blue and yellow.
But each unlike his fellow
Are the eggs of every hue.

And it's odd, as folk say,
That on no other day
In all of the whole year through,
Does this wonderful bunny,
So busy and funny,
Color eggs of every hue.

If this story you doubt
She will soon find you out,
And what do you think she will do?
On the next Easter morning
She'll bring you without warning,
Those eggs of every hue!

M. Josephine Todd

A SONG OF EASTER.

Sing, children, sing!
And the lily censers swing;
Sing that life and joy are waking and that Death no more is king.
Sing the happy, happy tumult of the slowly brightening Spring,
Sing, little children, sing!

Sing, children, sing!
Winter wild has taken wing.
Fill the air with the sweet tidings till the frosty echoes ring!
Along the eaves the icicles no longer glittering cling;
And the crocus in the garden lifts its bright face to the sun,
And in the meadows softly the brooks begin to run;
And the golden catkins swing
In the warm airs of the Spring;
Sing, little children, sing!

Sing, children, sing!
The lilies white you bring
In the joyous Easter morning for hope are blossoming;
And as the earth her shroud of snow from off her breast doth fling,
So may we cast our fetters off in God's eternal Spring.
So may we find release at last from sorrow and from pain,
So may we find our childhood's calm, delicious dawn again.
Sweet are your eyes, O little ones, that look with smiling grace,
Without a shade of doubt or fear into the Future's face!
Sing, sing in happy chorus, with joyful voices tell
That death is life, and God is good, and all things shall be well;
That bitter days shall cease
In warmth and light and peace,—
That Winter yields to Spring,—
Sing, little children, sing!

Celia Thaxter

THE WHITE HARE

Among the many customs which mark the observance of Easter Day, none is more widespread than that of colored eggs for the children. It originated in Germany, where the Easter hare is almost as important a figure in nursery lore as is St. Nicholas in that of Christmas. The children are taught to believe that if they are good and mind their parents, and are truthful and kind to one another, a snow-white hare will steal into the house on Easter Eve, when everybody is asleep, and secrete in odd corners any number of beautiful colored eggs for the good children, but none for the bad ones.

Has Gretchen been naughty? Has Hans been good? These are the questions which agitate their little minds all the evening, and when they are finally tucked into bed, it is not to sleep, but to watch for the white hare. But they never see him, for he is a very timid and wily animal, and not until they are fast asleep does he steal into the house.

They are out of bed at sunrise. How about the white hare? Has anybody seen it? No; but mother is certain she heard a noise, though father doubts whether they have been good enough for the white hare really to pay them a visit. However, they may look—perhaps in some odd corner he may have left an egg or two. The search begins—for a long time in vain—then finally an egg is found, a wonderful egg, a gorgeous egg, and then another and another, until there can be no doubt that the white hare thinks them very good children indeed.

This pretty custom has spread from Germany to England and America, and everywhere, on Easter morning, the children are searching for the proofs that the wonderful white hare loves them.

Anonymous

EASTER EGGS.

Dear Grandpa Lee, with little Grace,
   Followed the path-way to the mill;
Bright daisies starred the shady lane,
   And now and then a bird would trill.

Once, when a birdling spread its wings,
   She said, "All things are fair and gay,—
The sky so blue where birdie sings!"
   Said grandpa, "This is Easter Day."

Thus happily they onward went,
   Till Grace cried, "There is little Kate,
And Frank and Nellie, too—and oh!
   Nell's swinging on the garden gate!"

As Grace and grandpa came in sight,
   The little ones to meet them sped,—
Their eager, prattling lips apart,
   Eyes flashing bright and cheeks rose-red.

"Oh, grandpa! in the hedge we've found
   Four Easter eggs, all colored blue;
They're in the sweetest little nest;
   We want to show our prize to you!"

Said grandpa, "Touch them not, my dears;
   Those eggs God dyed with colors rare;
The mother-bird will soon come back,
   And guard her nest with loving care.

'These Easter eggs, in leaf-hid nests,
   Imprison countless song-birds bright,
That soon will break the tinted shell
   And rise and sing in joyous flight."

Clara W. Raymond

EASTER EGGS.

The custom of using eggs in various ways has always been connected with Easter, and at one time the making of presents of colored eggs was almost universal. The origin of the custom has been explained in a number of ways. From the remotest ages the egg has been looked upon as a symbol of creation or new birth. According to the Persians the world was hatched from an egg at the season of the year which corresponds to the spring equinox. Hence the Parsees still exchange gifts of colored eggs at the New Year's festival which they celebrate about this time. The Romans had egg games which they celebrated at the time of our Easter, with races on oval tracks and eggs for prizes. The early Christians considered the egg an emblem of the resurrection.

Nowhere is the Easter egg more used than in Russia. Here the people all carry eggs with them when they go out on Easter Sunday and present them to everyone they meet. In parts of England and continental Europe various Easter egg contests still survive. One game is to trundle eggs down a hill, those whose eggs reach the bottom unbroken being victorious over the others. This is probably the origin of the custom observed in our own cuntry. In Washington it has been customary since the beginning of the 19th century for the children to gather on the White House grounds every Easter Monday and roll eggs down the slope.

Artificial eggs made of sugar, etc., and enclosing candy or gifts have in recent years been superseding the genuine Easter egg.

Anonymous, 1913

May Day

May Day—the first of the month—is one of the most ancient of the world's festivals. Its observance today in the United States has declined over the years to the point that the day may pass completely unnoticed. It is basically a festival of flowers and revelry, a time for celebrating the full beauty of the Spring season. Only since 1889 has the day been identified at all with the international Socialist labor movement or, more recently, with the Communist party. Rather than affording an example of modern firepower or of union solidarity, May Day is traditionally the most gentle and peaceful of holidays.

The one tradition which has survived to modern times is the making and giving of May Day baskets. Usually cornucopias of paper with a handle, these simple gifts of Spring blossoms are hung on the doorknob of the front door of the recipient—a lonely lady down at the end of the street, a favorite friend next door, a relative across town. Children often make these tokens of friendship in school, as worthy a project as almost any other holiday-inspired activity.

The May Day traditions of Great Britain have reached North American shores, but most have not captured the popular imagination. The most imaginative of these customs is May-pole dancing. A large pole, often of supple birch, is erected in a playing field or green, and to it are attached multi-colored ribbons. Dancers circle the pole and wind the colorful bands around it. The participants continue their dancing around the decorated pole, sometimes executing fancy Morris dance steps, a form of group dancing which originated in medieval times. The high moment of the observance may be reached with the crowning of a queen of the May—a young girl who will wear a wreath of flowers and greens and preside over the festivities. Like Halloween, the day may be an occasion for fancy dress costumes and merrymaking on the part of strolling musicians and jesters. Poet John Milton described such a festive scene in early seventeenth-century England:

> Now the bright morning-star, day's harbinger,
> Comes dancing from the east, and leads with her
> The flowery May, who from her green lap throws
> The yellow cowslip and the pale primrose.
> Hail, bounteous May, that dost inspire
> Mirth and youth and warm desire!
> Woods and groves are of thy dressing,
> Hill and dale doth boast thy blessing.
> Thus we salute thee with our early song,
> And welcome thee, and wish thee long.

May Day is obviously not a religious festival in the modern sense. In fact, the event described by Milton was banned by the Puritans in England in 1644 and was not resumed until the Restoration of royal rule in the 1660s. Milton was himself a follower of the Puritan faith but was presumably not offended by the revelry which has its roots in the pagan rites of Rome and worship of the goddess Flora and of Maia from whom we derive the name of the month. Puritans in early America were similarly blue-nosed about May Day frolics. The destruction of a May pole in 1660 at Merrymount in Massachusetts by Governor Endicott and a band of militia men is recorded in one of Nathaniel Hawthorne's famous short stories.

Certain phrases and terms have come down to us from these early May celebrations. "Going-a-Maying" refers to the practice of gathering flowering branches in the woods for decorating doors and windows of the home and the bower in which the Queen of the May was enthroned. Most often the chosen boughs were hawthorn blooms which reached maturity around the 1st of May in the British Isles. Thus, the term "The May," has come to mean the hawthorn.

A revival of May Day festivities took place in America in the late nineteenth century at private women's colleges and secondary schools on the East Coast. These activities involve the dancing around a May pole, and sometimes the crowning of a queen. The participants often carry a chain of daisies, and the occasion may be used as an opportunity to present various athletic and scholarly awards to students. Athletic contests are sometimes scheduled for the day. Such festivities, however, have declined with the growing movement toward coeducation. Their very frivolity is thought by many to be at odds with the more serious aims of modern higher education. To be sure, there is nothing "educational" per se in such Springtime rites, but it seems a pity to dismiss them as without meaning and purpose. A festival day such as this reminds us of simple, immaterial pleasures that can be enjoyed by all. And it provides a welcome break in the work-a-day pursuit of profit. How nice it would be to turn back the clock and sing with the children of the nineteenth century:

> Sister, awake! close not your eyes!
> The day her light discloses,
> And the bright morning doth arise
> Out of her bed of roses.
> See the clear sun, the world's bright eye,
> In at our window peeping:
> Lo, how he blusheth to espy
> Us idle children sleeping!
> Therefore awake! make haste, I say
> And let us, without staying,
> All in our gowns of green so gay
> Into the park a-Maying!

GOING-A-MAYING

Oh! ring the bells, Oh! ring the bells!
  We bid you all, "Good morning";
Give thanks we pray, our flowers are gay,
  And fair for your adorning.

Oh! ring the bells, Oh! ring the bells!
  Good friends, accept our greetings;
Where we have been, the woods are green,
  And fast the Spring is fleeting.

Oh! ring the bells, Oh! ring the bells!
  For this fair time of Maying;
We blossoms bring, and while we sing,
  Oh! hark to what we're saying.

QUEEN OF THE MAY.

THE MAY QUEEN

You must wake and call me early, call me early, mother dear;
To-morrow 'ill be the happiest time of all the glad New-year;
Of all the glad New-year, mother, the maddest, merriest day,
For I'm to be Queen o' the May, mother, I'm to be Queen o' the May. . . .

I sleep so sound all night, mother, that I shall never wake,
If you do not call me loud when the day begins to break;
But I must gather knots of flowers, and buds and garlands gay,
For I'm to be Queen o' the May, mother, I'm to be Queen o' the May. . . .

Little Effie shall go with me to-morrow to the green,
And you'll be there, too, mother, to see me made the Queen;
For the shepherd lads on every side 'ill come from far away,
And I'm to be Queen o' the May, mother, I'm to be Queen o' the May. . . .

Alfred Lord Tennyson

A SONG FOR MAY DAY

Come out and join the revels!
  Don't mope the hours away
In dusty chimney corners;
  It's time to greet the May.

See April here rejoicing
  She's laid aside her gray,
Adorned herself with ribands,
  And flaunts a rich array.

Now clear your cheeks of sorrow
  And turn your thoughts to play.
The air is filled with music
  For Earth makes holiday.

Frederick Herbert Adler

MAY DAY MORNING

Oh, let's leave a basket of flowers today
For the little old lady who lives down our way!
We'll heap it with violets white and blue,
With a Jack-in-the-pulpit and windflowers too.

We'll make it of paper and line it with ferns,
Then hide—and we'll watch her surprise when she turns
And opens her door and looks out to see
Who in the world it could possibly be!

Virginia Scott Miner

THE MAY PARTY

O million-singing comes the May
   And whose dumb heart but wakes and thrills?
Now, as of old, the break-of-day
   Sings through the heart as through the hills—
New spirit and new day are born—
   Yea, in our souls great suns arise
With flame more glorious than the morn
   Lit with sun-centred skies!

O we have watched the blossoms slip
   Through hills of sunniest silent green,
And when at morn the bluebirds drip
   Dew on wet logs, our eyes have seen—
Yea, marked the unmowed meadow tremble
   Through a million blades of grass new-born—
Yea, heard the birds of song assemble
   The beauty of the morn!

But there is one thing I have seen
   That shall be held within the heart,
When all that deepens into green
   Or blooms in bright blue shall depart—

It was a hill that blossomed rich
   With buds of an all-lovelier hue
Than the wild spring-things that bewitch
   Each year our souls anew!

Lo, in the park, and up the lawn,
   And laughing in the leafiness,
And fresh with all the fragrant dawn,
   And dancing in gay gala dress,
Our city children loosed to skies,
   A thousand little souls laid bare
To all the gales of Paradise
   That wandered through their hair.

O loveliness more absolute
   Than bird or bough or beast or bud,
O pure sweet splendors that transmute
   May's unsoul'd marvellous full flood
Into a something lit with God!
   O gazing where they danced and ran
I knew then why earth's blossoming sod
   Had given birth to man!

James Oppenheim

Mother's Day

Considering the appropriateness of a special day reserved to honor Mother, the observance of Mother's Day itself is strictly a twentieth-century phenomenon, although the day does have dim antecedents in past history.

The historical source of Mother's Day, according to some commentators, is the ancient spring festivals dedicated by the worshippers of Cybele to the Great Mother of the Gods, the symbol of universal motherhood. She was the great parent of gods and men, as well as of the lower orders of creation. She was called the Mountain Mother; her sanctuaries were almost invariably upon mountains, and frequently in caves; lions were her faithful companions. Her special affinity with her wild nature was manifested by the orgiastic character of her worship. Her attendants, the Corybantes, were wild, half-demonic beings. Her priests, the Galli, were eunuchs attired in female garb, with long hair fragrant with ointment. Together with priestesses, they celebrated her rites with wild music and dancing until their frenzied excitement found its culmination in self-scourging, self-laceration, or exhaustion.

A bridge between this almost bacchanalian worship of the female principle of life and the honoring of our modern mothers may be Mid-Lent Sunday, also called "Mothering Sunday," which in years past was widely observed in England on the fourth Sunday after Lent. The early Church, in preserving some of the customs of pre-Christianity, may possibly have substituted for the Great Mother of the Gods either the Mother Church or the mother of Jesus, the Virgin Mary. Over the years the custom arose of students, apprentices, and servants returning home on Mothering Sunday with small gifts of bouquets of violets or of "mothering cake" for their mothers.

In 1864 Robert Chambers wrote of Mothering Sunday in his famous *Book of Days*, the grandfather of all books on holidays and festivals: "The harshness and general painfulness of life in old times must have been much relieved by certain simple and affectionate customs which modern people have learned to dispense with. Amongst these was a practice of going to see parents, and especially the female one, on the mid-Sunday of Lent, taking for them some little present, such as a cake or a trinket. A youth engaged in this amiable act of duty was said to go *a-mothering,* and thence the day itself came to be called Mothering Sunday. There was a cheering and peculiar festivity appropriate to the day, the prominent dish being *furmety*—which we have to interpret as wheat grains boiled in sweet milk, sugared and spiced. In the northern part of England, and in Scotland, there seems to have been a greater leaning to steeped pease fried in butter, with pepper and salt. Pancakes so composed passed by the name of *carlings*; and so conspicuous was this article, that from it Carling Sunday became a local name for the day."

Another name for "mothering cake" was "simnel cake," a rich plum-pudding ornamented with scallops and eaten in commemoration of the banquet given by the biblical Joseph to his brethren, which forms the first lesson of Mid-Lent Sunday, and the feeding of the five thousand, which forms the Gospel of the day.

The honor of originating the modern Mother's Day belongs to Miss Anna Jarvis of Philadelphia (1864–1948). Her mother, Mrs. Anna Reese Jarvis, a minister's daughter who taught Sunday school classes in her native town of Grafton, West Virginia, died in Philadelphia on May 9, 1906. On the first anniversary of her mother's death in 1907, Miss Jarvis told a friend whom she had invited to a memorial service of her desire to dedicate a day to all mothers. Before the next anniversary came, she had interested many individuals and organizations in the observance of the second Sunday in May as Mother's Day. As a result of her efforts, Philadelphia observed the day, May 10, 1908. Miss Jarvis then became the missionary of the idea. She interviewed many public men and pleaded for the observance of the day. She achieved spectacular success. By 1912, the governor of Texas was observing Mother's Day by pardoning a number of prisoners. In May, 1913, Pennsylvania made it a state holiday. On May 10th of the same year, a resolution passed the Senate and the House of Representatives to make the second Sunday in May a national holiday, "dedicated to the memory of the best mother in the world, your mother."

Through the years Miss Jarvis became the means of organizing a national and an international organization to further the promotion of the observance of Mother's Day. The holiday began to be observed in England, for example, as early as 1913. The second Sunday in May is observed in all churches irrespective of creed, and the previous Friday is generally observed in most public schools, especially by little children who bring home with them the artistic tokens created in class for Mother.

Mother's Day was intended originally to be "observed through some distinct act of kindness, visit, letter, gift, or tribute to show remembrance of the mother to whom general affection is due." For a time the day was observed as Father's Day, as well, "designed to perpetuate all family ties." But Father eventually earned a day for himself, just as Grandparents have in 1978. (See the chapter on Father's Day.) The slogan of the day is in honor of "the best mother who ever lived." The badge of the day is traditionally a carnation (Miss Jarvis's mother's favorite flower)—red for a living mother and white for one who has died.

In recent years Mother's Day, like so many other American holidays, has degenerated into a display of commercial gift-giving, heralded by merchants' advertisements in newspapers and magazines that seem to appear earlier each year. Anna Jarvis lived long enough to be disillusioned by the commercialism of the day she helped to bring about. Her spirit would seem to suggest that the United States economy would not be seriously affected if Mother were to be given sincere love and perhaps a handmade token or the bouquet of wild flowers so popular in the past. And, certainly, one custom of old-fashioned Mothering Sunday should be preserved: Mother's Day is a perfect time for a family reunion.

LITH. & PUB. BY N. CURRIER,   Entered according to Act of Congress in the year 1846 by N. Currier, in the Clerk's office of the District Court of the Southern District of New York.   2 SPRUCE ST. N.Y.

MOTHER AND CHILD.

THE FIRST
MOTHER'S DAY PROCLAMATION

WHEREAS, By a Joint Resolution approved May 8, 1914, "designating the second Sunday in May as Mother's Day, and for other purposes," the President is authorized and requested to issue a proclamation calling upon the government officials to display the United States flag on all government buildings, and the people of the United States to display the flag at their homes or other suitable places on the second Sunday in May as a public expression of our love and reverence for the mothers of our country:

AND WHEREAS, By the said Joint Resolution it is made the duty of the President to request the observance of the second Sunday in May as provided for in the said Joint Resolution:

Now, Therefore, I, Woodrow Wilson, President of the United States of America, by virtue of the authority vested in me by the said Joint Resolution, do hereby direct the government officials to display the United States flag on all government buildings and do invite the people of the United States to display the flag at their homes or other suitable places on the second Sunday in May as a public expression of our love and reverence for the mothers of our country.

MY MOTHER'S HANDS

My mother's hands are cool and fair,
   They can do anything.
Delicate mercies hide them there
   Like flowers in the spring.

When I was small and could not sleep,
   She used to come to me,
And with my cheek upon her hand
   How sure my rest would be!

For everything she ever touched
   Of beautiful or fine,
Their memories living in her hands
   Would warm that sleep of mine.

Her hands remember how they played
   One time in meadowy streams,—
And all the flickering song and shade
   Of water took my dreams.

Swift through her haunted fingers pass
   Memories of garden things;—
I dipped my face in flowers and grass
   And sounds of hidden wings.

One time she touched the cloud that kissed
   Brown pastures bleak and far:—
I leaned my head into a mist
   And thought I was a star.

All this was very long ago
   And I am grown; but yet
The hand that lured my slumber so
   I never can forget.

For still when drowsiness comes on
   It seems so soft and cool,
Shaped happily beneath my cheek,
   Hollow and beautiful.

Anna Hempstead Branch

STRANGE LANDS

Where do you come from, Mr. Jay?
"From the land of Play, from the land of Play."
And where can that be, Mr. Jay?
  "Far away—far away."

Where do you come from, Mrs. Dove?
"From the land of Love, from the land of Love."
And how do you get there, Mrs. Dove?
  "Look above—look above."

Where do you come from, Baby Miss?
"From the land of Bliss, from the land of Bliss."
And what is the way there, Baby Miss?
  "Mother's kiss—Mother's kiss."

Laurence Alma-Tadema

MY MOTHER

I knew her first as food and warmth and rest,
A silken lap, soft arms, a tender breast;
Then, as fear came into my world, I knew
She was a never-failing refuge too.
Then I discovered play—my playmate she,
Unwearied in gay ingenuity,
And yet at the same time in her I saw,
Scarce understood, and yet obeyed, the Law.
Time taught me more and more to comprehend
Her understanding sweetness as a friend,
And as my life's horizon grew more wide
Her meaning to myself was magnified
By vision that had grown at last to see
A love that could enfold the world—and me.
Oh, there were restive and impatient days
When wilful childhood craved its own wild ways
And flung aside the gently guiding hand—
Blind hours when I was slow to understand,
But Patience and a love that would not fail
Always prevailed—how could they but prevail?
And now so well I know her that I know
The graciousness of her spirit, and will be
Through all my life a radiant mystery
Since love like hers ever exceeds the sweep
Of mortal plummet, sound we ne'er so deep.
Eternity itself will not suffice
To fathom it. If all through Paradise
My mother's love shall lead me wondering,
Is God's a slighter and a shallower thing?
How shall I dare to dream that I enclose
Her Maker in the mind she overflows?

Amelia Josephine Burr

WHERE'S MOTHER?

Bright curly heads pop in all day
  To ask, "Is Mother here?"
Then give an eager glance around,
  And swiftly disappear.

She ought to wear a silver bell,
  Whose note, so sweet and clear,
Should tinkle out a cheery sound,
  Repeating, "Mother's near."

And then, if any little one
  Had something glad to tell,
Or scratches, bumps, or tears, or *tears,*
  Or secret woes befell,

No need to fly from room to room,
  But simply listen well,
And, like the happy little lambs,
  Just follow "Mother's" bell.

Sarah S. Baker.

THE WATCHER

She always leaned to watch for us,
   Anxious if we were late,
In winter by the window,
   In summer by the gate.

And though we mocked her tenderly,
   Who had such foolish care,
The long way home would seem more safe
   Because she waited there.

Her thoughts were all so full of us,
   She never could forget!
And so I think that where she is
   She must be watching yet,

Waiting till we come home to her,
   Anxious if we are late—
Watching from Heaven's window,
   Leaning from Heaven's gate.

Margaret Widdemer

ROCK ME TO SLEEP

Backward, turn backward, O Time, in your flight,
Make me a child again, just for to-night!
Mother, come back from the echoless shore,
Take me again to your heart as of yore;
Kiss from my forehead the furrows of care,
Smooth the few silver threads out of my hair;
Over my slumbers your loving watch keep;—
Rock me to sleep, mother,—rock me to sleep!

Backward, flow backward, O tide of the years!
I am so weary of toil and of tears,—
Toil without recompense, tears all in vain,—
Take them, and give me my childhood again!
I have grown weary of dust and decay,—
Weary of flinging my soul-wealth away;
Weary of sowing for others to reap;—
Rock me to sleep, mother,—rock me to sleep! . . .

Over my heart, in the days that have flown,
No love like mother-love ever has shown;
No other worship abides and endures,—
Faithful, unselfish, and patient, like yours:

None like a mother can charm away pain
From the sick soul and the world-weary brain.
Slumber's soft calms o'er my heavy lids creep;—
Rock me to sleep, mother,—rock me to sleep!

Come, let your brown hair, just lighted with gold,
Fall on your shoulders again as of old;
Let it drop over my forehead to-night,
Shading my faint eyes away from the light;
For from its sunny-edged shadows once more
Haply will throng the sweet visions of yore;
Lovingly, softly, its bright billows sweep;—
Rock me to sleep, mother,—rock me to sleep!

Mother, dear mother, the years have been long
Since I last listened your lullaby song:
Sing, then, and unto my soul it will seem
Womanhood's years have been only a dream.
Clasped to your heart in a loving embrace,
With your light lashes just sweeping my face,
Never hereafter to wake or to weep;—
Rock me to sleep, mother,—rock me to sleep!

Elizabeth Akers

Memorial Day

Memorial or Decoration Day came into being after the Civil War and until the 1900s was the occasion for honoring the dead of that great national tragedy. The date of May 30th was chosen by leaders of the Grand Army of the Republic, the Northern veterans' organization, as the observance day in 1868. By the 1880s every one of the Union states had set aside the day for various patriotic rites. In the South, a Confederate Memorial Day varies in date from as early as April 25th (Mississippi) to as late as June 3rd, also the birthday of Jefferson Davis (Kentucky, and Tennessee). In some of the border and Southern states, both the regular, May 30th, and a Confederate Memorial Day are observed. Where this is the case, the day devoted to memory of the Southern cause has been kept separate from that honoring the veterans of all wars. Although there is now a separate Veterans Day observance based on the former Armistice Day, the national observance of May 30th has come to include the honoring of all those who have fought in America's wars.

In its early years, Memorial Day was popularly known as Decoration Day, a descriptive term that is appropriate to the occasion. The major event of the observance was the decorating of graves—in the terms of the time, the "strewing" of flowers and garlands "or otherwise decorating the graves of comrades." It is thought that May 30th was chosen as the date because it was the anniversary of the discharge of the last Union volunteer of the war. Early observances of this sort were held as early as 1863 in the South at various times of the year. The campaign by the Grand Army of the Republic to officially establish such a day is credited to a story which appeared in Northern newspapers in 1867. It described the activity of "the women of Columbus, Mississippi, [who] have shown themselves impartial in their offerings made to the memory of the dead. They strewed flowers alike on the graves of the Confederate and of the National soldiers."

Throughout the North, posts of the G.A.R. spread the message of honoring their fallen brothers and of keeping alive the faith of the war years. John A. Logan, first Commander-in-Chief of the organization argued in his first proclamation inaugurating Memorial Day that the lives of "our heroic dead . . . were the reveille of freedom to a race in chains, and their death the tattoo of rebellious tyranny in arms. . . . Let us, then, at the time appointed, gather around their sacred remains and garland the passionless mounts above them with the choicest flowers of springtime; let us raise above them the dear old flag they saved from dishonor. . . ." The G.A.R. argued for years that *Memorial* Day was a much more appropriate and dignified term than *Decoration* Day.

The fires of passion fanned by the Civil War were so strong that it took years for them to subside—whether in the North or the South. Memorial Day, of course, was an occasion for much emotional outpouring, and it was perhaps a healthy expression of grief and fury over what had been lost on both sides. Sectional chauvinism played a part in most holiday proceedings throughout the nineteenth century, and undoubtedly parts of some ceremonies were downright offensive in their appeals to fear of the enemy, self-righteousness, and hatred. Unlike the practice in militaristic countries, these ceremonies—whether held after the Civil or Spanish-American wars or following one of the twentieth-century's major conflicts—were not an occasion for boastful displays of military might and right. Memorial Day was and is a day of mourning and remembering, of reconciling the past and present, and of hoping for a better future.

In the twentieth century Memorial Day also assumed an air of quiet celebration. In small towns throughout the country, school children gather as classroom units, Boy and Girl Scouts, Brownies and Cubs, marching bands and twirlers to lead a procession of adults to ceremonies at local cemeteries. Veterans of the Civil War or the Spanish-American War have long since disappeared from view, but their place has been taken by bands of World War I, II, Korean War, and Vietnam War comrades. Some are members of American Legion posts; others are from the Veterans of Foreign Wars or are representatives of the Disabled Veterans of America. They are joined by Waves, Wacs, Wafs, members of the women's auxiliaries of veterans' organizations, and such special units as the Gold Star Mothers. And, of course, there are the inevitable fire trucks, police cars, and, last, but not least, two or three stray dogs. This is no joyous 4th of July celebration, but neither is it a morose occasion. The step is as sprightly as age will allow, and the spring flowers carried by the children add a colorful and fragrant note to the day.

All Memorial Day ceremonies end at the cemetery where graves of veterans are marked by a flag. Here prayers are said by local clergy and words of consolation and wisdom pronounced by area dignitaries. When a twenty-one gun salute and taps is sounded, this peaceful and perhaps most thoughtful of American holiday celebrations is brought to an end. It is a long way from the roaring track of the Indy 500, also celebrated on this day each year. Memorial Day is an event of community feeling and pride which can in no way be replaced by the long-distance parlor games of television.

DECORATION DAY

How quickly Nature takes possession of a deserted battlefield, and goes to work repairing the ravages of man! With invisible magic hand she smooths the rough earthworks, fills the rifle-pits with delicate flowers, and wraps the splintered tree-trunks with her fluent drapery of tendrils. Soon the whole sharp outline of the spot is lost in unremembering grass. Where the deadly rifle-ball whistled through the foliage, the robin or the thrush pipes its tremulous note; and where the menacing shell described its curve through the air, a harmless crow flies in circles. Season after season the gentle work goes on, healing the wounds and rents made by the merciless enginery of war, until at last the once hotly contested battle-ground differs from none of its quiet surroundings, except, perhaps, that here the flowers take a richer tint and the grasses a deeper emerald.

It is thus the battle lines may be obliterated by Time, but there are left other and more lasting relics of the struggle. That dinted army saber, with a bit of faded crêpe knotted at its hilt, which hangs over the mantel-piece of the "best room" of many a town and country house in these States, is one; and the graven headstone of the fallen hero is another. The old swords will be treasured and handed down from generation to generation as priceless heirlooms, and with them, let us trust, will be cherished the custom of dressing with annual flowers the resting-places of those who fell during the Civil War.

The impulse which led us to set apart a day for decorating the graves of our soldiers sprung from the grieved heart of the nation, and in our own time there is little chance of the rite being neglected. But the generations that come after us should not allow the observance to fall into disuse. What with us is an expression of fresh love and sorrow should be with them an acknowledgment of an incalculable debt.

Decoration Day is the most beautiful of our national holidays. How different from those sullen batteries which used to go rumbling through our streets are the crowds of light carriages, laden with flowers and greenery, wending their way to the neighboring cemeteries! The grim cannon have turned into palm branches, and the shell and shrapnel into peach blooms. There is no hint of war in these gay baggage trains, except the presence of men in undress uniforms, and perhaps here and there an empty sleeve to remind one of what has been. Year by year that empty sleeve is less in evidence.

The observance of Decoration Day is unmarked by that disorder and confusion common enough with our people in their holiday moods. The earlier sorrow has faded out of the hour, leaving a softened solemnity It quickly ceased to be simply a local commemoration. While the sequestered country churchyards and burial-places near our great northern cities were being hung with May garlands, the thought could not but come to us that there were graves lying southward above which bent a grief as tender and sacred as our own. Invisibly we dropped unseen flowers upon these mounds. There is a beautiful significance in the fact that, two years after the close of the war, the women of Columbus, Mississippi, laid their offerings alike on Northern and Southern graves. When all is said, the great Nation has but one heart.

Thomas Bailey Aldrich.
From "Ponkapog Papers."

116

THE FIRST MEMORIAL DAY ADDRESS AT ARLINGTON NATIONAL CEMETERY, 1868

I am oppressed with a sense of the impropriety of uttering words on this occasion. If silence is ever golden, it must be here beside the graves of fifteen thousand men whose lives were more significant than speech and whose death was a poem the music of which can never be sung. With words we make promises, plight faith, praise virtue. Promises may not be kept; plighted faith may be broken; and vaunted virtue be only the cunning mask of vice. We do not know one promise these men made, one pledge they gave, one word they spoke; but we do know they summed up and perfected, by one supreme act, the highest virtues of men and citizens. For love of country they accepted death, and thus resolved all doubts, and made immortal their patriotism and virtue.

For the noblest man that lives, there still remains a conflict. He must still withstand the assaults of time and fortune, must still be assailed by temptations, before which lofty natures have fallen; but with these the conflict ended, the victory was won when death stamped on them the great seal of heroic character, and closed a record which years can never blot.

I know of nothing more appropriate on this occasion than to inquire what brought these men here; what high motive led them to condense life into an hour and to crown that hour by joyfully welcoming death. Let us consider.

Eight years ago this was the most unwarlike nation of the earth. For nearly fifty years no spot in any of these states had been the scene of battle. Thirty millions of people had an army of less than ten thousand men. The faith of our people in the stability and permanence of their institutions was like their faith in the eternal course of nature. Peace, liberty, and personal security were blessings as common and universal as sunshine and showers and fruitful seasons; and all sprang from a single source, the old American principle that all owe due submission and obedience to the lawfully expressed will of the majority. This is not one of the doctrines of our political system—it is the system itself. It is our political firmament, in which all other truths are set, as stars in heaven. It is the encasing air, the breath of the nation's life.

Against the principle the whole weight of the rebellion was thrown. Its overthrow would have brought such ruin as might follow in the physical universe if the power of gravitation were destroyed. . . .

As a flash of lightning in a midnight tempest reveals the abysmal horrors of the sea, so did the flash of the first gun disclose the awful abyss into which rebellion was ready to plunge us. In a moment we were the most warlike nation on earth. In a moment we were not merely a people with an army—we were a people in arms. The nation was in column—not all at the front, but all in array. I love to believe that no heroic sacrifice is ever lost; that the characters of men are molded and inspired by what their fathers have done; that treasured up in American souls are all the unconscious influences of the great deeds of the Anglo-Saxon race, from Agincourt to Bunker Hill. It was such an influence that led a young Greek, two thousand years ago, when musing on the battlefield of Marathon, to exclaim,

"The trophies of Militiades will not let me sleep!"

Could these men be silent in 1861; these whose ancestors have felt the inspiration of battle on every field where civilization had fought in the last thousand years? Read their answer in this green turf. Each for himself gathered up the cherished purposes of life—its aims and ambitions, its dearest affections—and flung all, with life itself, into the scale of battle. And now consider this silent assembly of the dead. What does it represent? Nay, rather, what does it not represent? It is an epitome of the war. Here are sheaves reaped in the harvest of death from every battlefield of Virginia. If each grave had a voice to tell us what its silent tenant last saw and heard on earth we might stand, with uncovered heads, and hear the whole story of the war. . . .

What other spot so fitting for their last resting place as this, under the shadow of the Capitol saved by their valor? Here, where the grim edge of battle joined; here, where all the hope and fear and agony of their country centered; here let them rest, asleep on the nation's heart, entombed in the nation's love.

General James A. Garfield,
later President of the United States

THE LEGACY OF CONFLICT

The captains and the armies who, after long years of dreary campaigning and bloody, stubborn fighting, brought to a close the Civil War, have left us even more than a reunited realm. The material effect of what they did is shown in the fact that the same flag flies from the Great Lakes to the Rio Grande, and all the people of the United States are richer because they are one people and not many, because they belong to one great nation and not to a contemptible knot of struggling nationalities.

But besides this, besides the material results of the Civil War, we are all, North and South, incalculably richer for its memories. We are the richer for each grim campaign, for each hard-fought battle. We are the richer for valor displayed alike by those who fought so valiantly for the right, and by those who, no less valiantly, fought for what they deemed the right. We have in us nobler capacities for what is great and good because of the infinite woe and suffering and because of the splendid ultimate triumph.

Theodore Roosevelt.

From "American Ideals."

THE BLUE
AND THE GRAY

By the flow of the inland river,
   Whence the fleets of iron have fled,
Where the blades of the grave-grass quiver,
   Asleep are the ranks of the dead:
     Under the sod and the dew,
       Waiting the Judgment Day:
     Under the one, the blue;
       Under the other, the Gray.

These in the robings of glory,
   Those in the gloom of defeat,
All with the battle-blood gory,
   In the dusk of eternity meet:
     Under the sod and the dew,
       Waiting the Judgment Day:
     Under the laurel, the Blue;
       Under the willow, the Gray.

From the silence of sorrowful hours
   The desolate mourners go,
Lovingly laden with flowers,
   Alike for the friend and the foe:
     Under the sod and the dew,
       Waiting the Judgment Day:
     Under the roses, the Blue;
       Under the lilies, the Gray.

So, with an equal splendor,
   The morning sun-rays fall,
With a touch impartially tender,
   On the blossoms blooming for all:
     Under the sod and the dew,
       Waiting the Judgment Day:
     Broidered with gold, the Blue;
       Mellowed with gold, the Gray. . . .

No more shall the war-cry sever,
   Or the winding rivers be red;
They banish our anger forever
   When they laurel the graves of our dead!
     Under the sod and the dew,
       Waiting the Judgment Day:
     Love and tears for the Blue;
       Tears and love for the Gray.

Francis Miles Finch

MEMORIAL DAY

From out our crowded calendar
   One day we pluck to give;
It is the day the Dying pause
   To honor those who live.

McLandburgh Wilson

DECORATION DAY

Sleep, comrades, sleep and rest
   On this Field of the Grounded Arms,
Where foes no more molest,
   Nor sentry's shot alarms!

Ye have slept on the ground before,
   And started to your feet
At the cannon's sudden roar,
   Or the drum's redoubling beat.

But in this camp of Death
   No sound your slumber breaks;
Here is no fevered breath,
   No wound that bleeds and aches.

All is repose and peace;
   Untrampled lies the sod;
The shouts of battle cease,
   It is the truce of God!

Rest, comrades, rest and sleep!
   The thoughts of men shall be
As sentinels to keep
   Your rest from danger free.

Your silent tents of green
   We deck with fragrant flowers;
Yours has the suffering been,
   The memory shall be ours.

Henry Wadsworth Longfellow

"BELLIGERENT NON-COMBATANTS"

It is related of General Scott that when he asked, in 1861, the probable length of the then Civil War, he answered, "The conflict of arms will last five years; but will be followed by twenty years of angry strife, by the 'belligerent non-combatants.' "

Wars are usually made by civilians, bold and defiant in the forum; but when the storm comes, they go below, and leave their innocent comrades to catch the "peltings of the pitiless storm." Of the half-million of brave fellows whose graves have this day been strewn with flowers, not one in a thousand had the remotest connection with the causes of the war which led to their untimely death. I now hope and beg that all good men, North and South, will unite in real earnest to repair the mistakes and wrongs of the past; will persevere in the common effort to make this great land of ours to blossom as the garden of Eden!

I invoke all to heed well the lessons of this "Decoration Day," to weave each year a fresh garland for the grave of some beloved comrade or hero, and to rebuke any and all who talk of civil war, save as the "last dread tribunal of kings and peoples."

William Tecumseh Sherman

From Decoration Day Address, New York, May 30, 1878

THE SOUTHERN SOLDIER

You of the North have had drawn for you with a master's hand the picture of your returning armies. You have heard how, in the pomp and circumstance of war, they came back to you, marching with proud and victorious tread, reading their glory in a nation's eyes. Will you bear with me while I tell you of another army that sought its home at the close of the late war—an army that marched home in defeat and not in victory, in pathos and not in splendor?

Let me picture to you the footsore Confederate soldier, as, buttoning up in his faded gray jacket the parole which was the testimony to his children of his fidelity and faith, he turned his face southward from Appomattox in April, 1865. Think of him as ragged, half-starved, heavy-hearted, enfeebled by want and wounds; having fought to exhaustion, he surrenders his gun, wrings the hands of his comrades in silence, and lifting his tear-stained and pallid face for the last time to the graves that dot the old Virginia hills, pulls his gray cap over his brow and begins the slow and painful journey.

What does he find—let me ask you, who went to your homes eager to find, in the welcome you had justly earned, full payment for four years' sacrifice—what does he find when, having followed the battle-stained cross against overwhelming odds, dreading death not half as much as surrender, he reaches the home he left so prosperous and beautiful?

He finds his house in ruins, his farms devastated, his stock killed, his barns empty, his trade destroyed, his money worthless; his social system, feudal in its magnificence, swept away; his people without law or legal status, his comrades slain, and the burdens of others heavy on his shoulders. Crushed by defeat, his very traditions are gone; without money, credit, employment, material or training.

What does he do—this hero in gray, with a heart of gold? Does he sit down in sullenness and despair?

Not for a day. Surely God, who had stripped him in his prosperity, inspired him in his adversity. As ruin was never so overwhelming, never was restoration swifter. The soldier stepped from the trenches, into the furrow; horses that had charged Federal guns marched before the plow, and fields that ran red with blood in April were green with the harvest in June.

Never was nobler duty confided to human hands than the uplifting and upbuilding of the prostrate and bleeding South, misguided, perhaps, but beautiful in her suffering. In the record of her social, industrial, and political evolution, we await with confidence the verdict of the world.

Henry W. Grady.

THE SOLDIER'S DIRGE

Dead in the battle,—dead on the field;
More than his life can a soldier yield?
Dead for his country, muffle the drums:
Slowly the sad procession comes.
The heart may ache, but the heart must swell
With pride for the soldier who fought so well.
His blood has burnished his sabre bright:
To his memory, honor; to him, good-night.

Elizabeth Harman

Flag Day

Although several different flags were unfurled at one time or another throughout early American history, it was not until June 14, 1777, that Congress, sitting in Philadelphia, adopted a resolution declaring "that the flag of the United States shall be of thirteen stripes of alternate red and white, with a union of thirteen stars of white in a blue field, representing the new constellation." The resolution was adopted following the reception of the report of a special committee appointed to suggest a design for the flag. A contemporary description of the design indicates that "The stars of the flag represent a new constellation rising in the West. The idea is taken from the great constellation Lyra, which in the hands of Orpheus, signifies harmony. The blue in the field is taken from the edge of the Covenanters Banner of Scotland, significant of the covenant of the United States against oppression. The stars are disposed in a circle, symbolizing the perpetuity of the Union, the ring signifying eternity. The thirteen stars show the number of the united colonies and denote subordination of the States of the Union as well as equality among themselves. The red, the color which in the Roman days was a symbol of defiance, denotes daring, and the white purity."

The popular tradition—long disproved, but persisting nonetheless—that a committee composed of George Washington, Robert Morris, and George Ross called upon Betsy Ross of Philadelphia and commissioned her to make the first flag is now regarded as of very doubtful authenticity. There is no contemporary evidence that any of these men or Mrs. Ross had any direct connection with making or designing the flag. (The person most probably associated with the creation of the first flag of the United States—Francis Hopkinson of New Jersey—is hardly likely to engender any popular legends of the future.) The Betsy Ross legend was first heard in 1870 when her grandson, William J. Canby, related this "family tradition" to the Pennsylvania Historical Society.

Equally fictitious is the legend regarding the shape of the stars on the American flag. According to this story, George Washington's committee insisted that the flag include six-pointed stars, but Mrs. Ross pointed out that a five-pointed star would be more attractive than one with six points. The committee, the story goes, reminded her that a great many flags would be required and that a five-pointed star was difficult to cut. Betsy Ross, in reply, took a piece of paper, folded it deftly, and with one snip of her scissors cut a perfect five-pointed star. Questionable, as well, are the words credited to George Washington about the origin of the flag's colors: "We take the stars from heaven, the red from our mother country, separating it by white stripes, thus showing that we have separated from her, and the white stripes shall go down to posterity, representing her liberty."

Among the earliest Stars and Stripes on record are the Bennington flag, present at the Battle of Bennington on August 16, 1777, and flags raised at the battles of Cooch's Bridge in Delaware, September 3, 1777, and Brandywine in Pennsylvania, September 11, 1777.

The very first flag of the United States of America may well have been the "hurry up" or "home-made" Stars and Stripes that was improvised and floated over Fort Schuyler at Rome, New York, on August 2, 1777. Among the makers of this flag was Col. Marinus Willett, and his story is supported by historical evidence. In a contemporary letter, a British soldier wrote that "Over the Fort Stanwix built by us in 1758 and named after the brave General Stanwix, they [the Americans] hoisted a flag of white and red stripes and on a canton of azure there were white stars." Colonel Willett's diary and narrative reads as follows: "The fort [Fort Stanwix] had never been supplied with a flag. The necessity of having one had, upon the arrival of the enemy, taxed the invention of the garrison a little; and a decent one was soon contrived. The white stripes were cut out of an ammunition shirt; the blue out of the camlet cloak taken from the enemy at Peekskill, while the red stripes were made of different pieces of the stuff procured from one and another of the garrison." Another witness of the garrison wrote in his letters home that "The blue ground for the stars was composed of a cloth cloak belonging to Captain Abraham Swartout of Dutchess County." The captain may therefore have worn the camlet cloak taken from the British at the Battle of Peekskill.

On the admission of Vermont in 1791, the citizens complained that their new state was not represented in the flag in either star or stripe. Then in 1792 Kentucky also joined the Union, and she, like Vermont, was not symbolized with the star or stripe, and so it can be said that these two states were without heraldic representation on the national flag until May, 1795, when Congress ordered: "That from and after the first day of May 1795 the flag of the United States be 15 stripes, alternate red and white; and that the union be 15 stars, white in a blue field."

But this did not solve the problem of flag standardization, for in 1796 Tennessee came into the Union and wished a star and a stripe, as did also Ohio in 1802; Louisiana in 1812; Indiana in 1816; Mississippi in 1817; and Illinois in 1818. In order that all new states in the future would not insist on both stars and stripes, Congress ordered in 1818 "That from and after the fourth day of July next, the flag of the United States be 13 horizontal stripes, alternate red and white;" and "That on the admission of every new State into the Union, one star be added to the union of the flag; and that such addition shall take effect on the fourth of July next succeeding such admission."

The meaning of the flag of the United States was perhaps best phrased by Woodrow Wilson at the Flag Day celebration at the White House in 1914: "This flag for the future is meant to stand for the just use of undisputed national power. No nation is ever going to doubt our power to assert its rights, and we should lay it to heart that no nation shall ever henceforth doubt our purpose to put it to the highest uses to which a great emblem of justice and government can be put.

"It is henceforth to stand for self-possession, for dignity, for the assertion of the right of one nation to serve the other nations of the world—an emblem that will not condescend to be used for purposes of aggression and self-aggrandizement; that is too great to be debased by selfishness; that has vindicated its right to be honored by all nations of the world and feared by none who do righteousness."

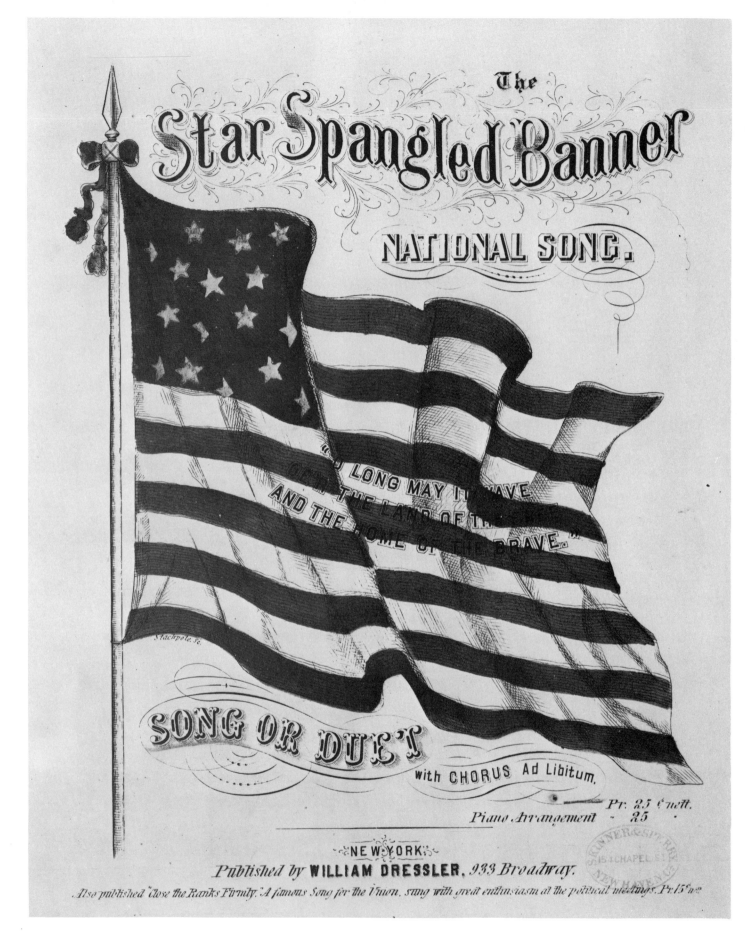

THE STAR-SPANGLED BANNER

Oh! say, can you see, by the dawn's early light,
   What so proudly we hailed at the twilight's last gleaming?
Whose broad stripes and bright stars through the perilous fight,
   O'er the ramparts we watched were so gallantly streaming;
And the rocket's red glare, the bombs bursting in air,
Gave proof through the night that our flag was still there;
   Oh! say, does that star-spangled banner yet wave
   O'er the land of the free and the home of the brave?

On the shore, dimly seen through the mists of the deep,
   Where the foe's haughty host in dread silence reposes,
What is that which the breeze, o'er the towering steep,
   As it fitfully blows, now conceals, now discloses?
Now it catches the gleam of the morning's first beam,
In full glory reflected, now shines on the stream;
   'Tis the star-spangled banner! oh, long may it wave
   O'er the land of the free and home of the brave!

And where are the foes who so vauntingly swore
   That the havoc of war and the battle's confusion
A home and a country should leave us no more?
   Their blood has washed out their foul footsteps' pollution.
No refuge could save the hireling and slave
From the terror of death and the gloom of the grave;
   And the star-spangled banner in triumph doth wave
   O'er the land of the free and the home of the brave!

Oh! thus be it ever, when freemen shall stand
   Between their loved homes and the war's desolation;
Blest with victory and peace, may the heaven-rescued land
   Praise the power that hath made and preserved us a nation.
Then conquer we must, when our cause it is just,
And this be our motto, "In God is our trust."
   And the star-spangled banner in triumph shall wave
   O'er the land of the free and the home of the brave!

Francis Scott Key

OUR FLAG

Only a bit of color
  Waving upon the street;
Only a wind-whipped pennant
  Where the band plays shrill and sweet.

Yet the soldier's heart beats faster,
  And proud is the sailor's eye,
And the citizen's step is quickened
  When our flag is passing by.

Only a bit of color,
  Did I hear a body say?
True be the hearts that greet it
  Wherever it waves today!

Back of that bit of color
  Lies a nation's history,
And ahead of our splendid banner—
  Who knows what there yet may be?

Frances Crosby Hamlet

BETSY'S BATTLE FLAG

From dusk till dawn the livelong night
She kept the tallow dips alight,
And fast her nimble fingers flew
To sew the stars upon the blue.
With weary eyes and aching head
She stitched the stripes of white and red,
And when the day came up the stair
Complete across a carven chair
  Hung Betsy's battle flag.

Like shadows in the evening gray
The Continentals filed away,
With broken boots and ragged coats,
But hoarse defiance in their throats;
They bore the marks of want and cold,
And some were lame and some were old,
And some with wounds untended bled,
But floating bravely overhead
  Was Betsy's battle flag.

When fell the battle's leaden rain,
The soldier hushed his moans of pain
And raised his dying head to see
King George's troopers turn and flee.
Their charging column reeled and broke,
And vanished in the rolling smoke,
Before the glory of the stars,
The snowy stripes, and scarlet bars
  Of Betsy's battle flag.

Minna Irving

THE NATIONAL BANNER

All hail to our glorious ensign!
courage to the heart, and strength to the hand,
to which, in all times, it shall be entrusted!
May it ever wave in honor, in unsullied glory, and patriotic hope,
on the dome of the capitol, on the country's stronghold,
on the entented plain, on the wave-rocked topmast.
Wherever, on the earth's surface,
the eye of the American shall behold it, may he have reason to bless it.
On whatsoever spot it is planted,
there may freedom have a foothold, humanity a brave champion,
and religion an altar.
Though stained with blood in a righteous cause,
may it never in any cause be stained with shame.
Alike, when its gorgeous folds
shall wanton in lazy holiday-triumphs on the summer breeze,
and its tattered fragments be dimly seen through the clouds of war,
may it be the joy and pride
of the American heart.
First raised in the cause of right and liberty,
in that cause alone may it forever spread
out its streaming blazonry to the battle and the storm.
Having been borne victoriously across the continent
and on every sea, may virtue and freedom and peace
forever follow where it leads the way.

Edward Everett

I AM THE FLAG

I am a composite being of all the people of America.

I am the union if you are united.

I am one and indivisible if you are undivided.

I am as strong as the weakest link.

I am an emblem of your country.

I am a symbol of a shadow of the real.

I am a sign pointing to past achievements.

I am a promise of greater things for the future.

I am what you make me.

I am purity if you are pure.

I am bravery if you are brave.

I am loyalty if you are loyal.

I am prosperity if you are prosperous.

I am honor if you are honorable.

I am goodness if you are good.

I am hope if you are hopeful.

I am truth if you are true. I have not always been truth, for you were not always true. You boasted of the "land of the free and the home of the brave" when your boast was a half lie.

I was deceived because you deceived yourselves.

I am the Constitution.

I am law and order.

I am tolerance or intolerance as you force me to be.

I am liberty as you understand liberty.

I am as a pillar of fire by night, but you must provide the fuel.

I march at the head of the column, but you must carry me on.

I have marched across the continent from ocean to ocean during my young life, and watched the growth of a nation from fewer than three million to more than one hundred million, because you encouraged and forced me to do so.

I stand for greater and more glorious achievement than can be found in recorded history, but you must be my inspiration.

I AM THE FLAG.

Lawrence M. Jones

THE EAGLE'S SONG

The lioness whelped, and the sturdy cub
Was seized by an eagle and carried up,
And homed for a while in an eagle's nest,
And slept for a while on an eagle's breast;
And the eagle taught it the eagle's song:
"To be staunch, and valiant, and free, and strong!"

The lion-whelp sprang from the eyrie nest,
From the lofty crag where the queen birds rest;
He fought the King on the spreading plain,
And drove him back o'er the foaming main.
He held the land as a thrifty chief,
And reared his cattle, and reaped his sheaf,
Nor sought the help of a foreign hand,
Yet welcomed all to his own free land!

Two were the sons that the country bore
To the Northern lakes and the Southern shore;
And Chivalry dwelt with the Southern son,
And Industry lived with the Northern one.
Tears for the time when they broke and fought!
Tears was the price of the Union wrought!
And the land was red in a sea of blood,
Where brother for brother had swelled the flood!

And now that the two are one again,
Behold on their shield the word, "Refrain!"
And the lion cub twain sing the eagle's song:
"To be staunch, and valiant, and free, and strong!"
For the eagle's beak, and the lion's paw,
And the lion's fangs, and the eagle's claw,
And the eagle's swoop, and the lion's might,
And the lion's leap, and the eagle's sight,
Shall guard the flag with the word "Refrain!"
Now that the two are one again!

Richard Mansfield

Father's Day

Of Father's Day, Robert J. Myers writes in *Celebrations*: "Modern America appears to be unique in its honoring of fathers on a special day. The observance most similar to our Father's Day was the ancient Roman Parentalia, which lasted from the thirteenth of February to the twenty-second. This festival, however, was not for living fathers, but was rather a time of remembrance, commemorating departed parents and kinsfolk. The ceremonies were held, Ovid says, to 'appease the souls of your fathers.' This annual observance became a family reunion. Members offered wine, honey, oil, and water at the flower-decorated graves. At the concluding ceremony, known as the Caristia, much celebrating went on as the living relatives feasted together, having been cleansed by the performance of their duties to the dead."

The modern American Father's Day is a development of the twentieth century, having come into being in that same period that gave rise to Mother's Day although its general acceptance was a bit slower in coming. Several people, each without knowledge of the others, were instrumental in bringing about the institution of Father's Day. On July 5, 1908, at the suggestion of Mrs. Charles Clayton, Dr. Robert T. Webb held a special service commemorating fathers at the Central Church of Fairmont, West Virginia; four years later, the people of Vancouver, Washington, believing their celebration to be the first, honored fathers at the suggestion of Reverend J. H. Berringer, pastor of the Irvington Methodist Church; in 1915, Harry C. Meek, who believed that he originated the idea, began pressing for a Father's Day in speeches made before Lions Clubs throughout the country. The Lions, in fact, were the first to suggest the date of the third Sunday in June as Father's Day. But Father's Day's most enthusiastic promoter was Mrs. John Bruce Dodd of Spokane, Washington. The idea of a special day for fathers occurred to Mrs. Dodd while listening to a sermon on Mother's Day, 1909. Since she and her five brothers had been raised on a Washington farm by her father after her mother's death, she saw the day as a suitable tribute to the indefatigable efforts not only of her own father, but of fathers everywhere. Through Mrs. Dodd's efforts, Spokane celebrated the first Father's Day in June, 1910, and Washington became the first state to recognize the day.

Although all presidents from Woodrow Wilson on have participated in celebrations or annual proclamations honoring father, Father's Day was finally established permanently in 1972, when President Richard M. Nixon, signing a Congressional resolution, designated the third Sunday in June as a national holiday: Father's Day.

Much has been written about the importance of fathers, but few passages are more memorable than the words delivered in 1961 by Adlai E. Stevenson before the National Father's Day Committee. They should become part of the national treasury of meaningful prose:

"Now it has been said that paternity is a career imposed on you one fine morning without any inquiry as to your fitness for it. That is why there are so many fathers who have children but so few children who have fathers.

"Is there truth or cynicism in this remark? A bit of both, I imagine, but far too much of the former for my taste.

"It is an all too visible truth that fatherhood is no longer the sacred duty it was once held to be. There are, today, far too many absentee fathers, fathers in name only. Paradoxically, and this is an insight into the nature of contemporary society, they are, in many cases, men whose ability, sense of responsibility, and moral integrity outside the home are of the first order.

"Apologists for these errant progenitors (in most instances, offenders themselves) have called up a multitude of rationalizations in their defense—two world wars in less than half a century, the pressures of modern urban life, business before pleasure, country before self, and other tired old saws.

"What nonsense. There is absolutely no excuse for a parent to abdicate his most important duty—the proper raising of his children. No father should be allowed to get away with the cowardly logic which concludes that his only job in the family is to pay for the bacon. His role is much more grandiose than that. If it is to be properly fulfilled, he should be, in his realm, a man of many faces—an artist, a philosopher, a statesman, and, above all, a prolific dispenser of good sense and justice.

"But it is vitally important, especially in the early years, that his children see in father a working model of the social order in which, not so many years hence, they will be expected to play a dynamic part.

"How can we, the parents, hope to secure a just and rational society if we neglect the development of those very instruments, our children, most necessary for its implementation? What good does it do to conceive grand moral, social, or political plans for a better world if the children who will have to live them out fail to see their importance?

"In a very real sense, a father's relations with his children should be a microcosmic reflection of their relations with the society in which they live. Through his actions a father must teach his children the intrinsic meaning of the democratic concept—freedom with restraint and the nature of integrity. "

Let us, then, dedicate the third Sunday in June to father, not least in recognition of his role as the wellspring of integrity.

LOOK AT PAPA.

FATHER'S DAY

He never talks of love or trust:
   Just gives my hand a pat,
But he would give his life for me,
   For Dads are made like that.

Though I am foolish, cruel, cross,
   He does not reprimand.
My other friends may turn aside
   But Dad will understand.

The brilliant ties or wrong-size sox
   Are trivial gifts I bring.
But Dad just reads my inmost thoughts:
   He knows he reigns as king.

—Vivian Orden Reeves

MY OLD MAN

When I was a boy of 14, my father was so ignorant I could hardly stand to have the old man around. But when I got to be 21, I was astonished at how much the old man had learned in seven years.

Mark Twain

FATHERS

Who is it wears the patch-work hose,
And seldom goes to picture shows,
That his little girl may have fine clothes?
It's *Father*.

Who is it wears last summer's hat,
That his boy might be in a sporty frat,
And thinks it's quite all right at that?
It's *Father*.

We've Mothers' Day and Poppy Day,
And lots of other holidays,
But almost all are Labor Days,
For *Father*.

Get out his slippers and easy chair,
Caress and smooth his rumpled hair,
And let him know you're glad he's there—
Your *Father*.

Anonymous

MY FATHER

Who in my Childhood's earliest day,
Before my tongue one word could say,
Would let me with his watch-chain play,
My Father.

When seated on my Mother's knee,
Who used to play at peep with me
Hiding, where Baby could not see?
My Father.

Who coaxed me, physic for to take,
Giving me sugar plums and cake,
If I would drink it for his sake?
My Father.

Who placed me on his foot to ride
While anxiosly my Mother cried,
To hold her Boy lest he should slide,
My Father.

WHAT TO TELL A CHILD
WHO ASKS "WHY?"

Nothing can be more fatal to your discipline than to allow your children to contradict you. If you happen to be betrayed into any misstatement or exaggeration in their presence, don't permit them to correct you.

Right or wrong, you must obstinately insist on your own infallibility, and promptly suppress every symptom of puerile skepticism, with force if need be. The moment you permit them to doubt your unerring wisdom, you will begin to forfeit their respect and pander to their conceit . . . I vividly remember how my father who was one of the most rigid and successful of disciplinarians—quelled the aspiring egotism that prompted me to correct his careless remark (when he was reckoning a problem . . .) that five times twelve was sixty-two and a half. "So," said he, climbing over his spectacles and surveying me grimly, "ye think ye know more 'n yer father, hey? Come 'ere to me!" His invitation was too pressing to be declined, and for a few excruciating moments I reposed in bitter humiliation across his left knee, with my neck in the embrace of his left arm.

I didn't see him demonstrate his mathematical accuracy, with the palm of his right hand on the largest patch of my trousers, but I *felt* that the old man was right; and when, after completely eradicating my faith in the multiplication-table, he asked me how much five times twelve was, I insisted, with tears in my eyes, that it was sixty-two and a half. "That's right!" said he; "I'll larn ye to respect yer father, if I have to thrash ye twelve times a day. Now go 'n water them hosses, 'n be lively too!" The old gentleman didn't permit any respect for him to wane much until the inflammatory rheumatism disabled him; and even then he continued to inspire me with awe until I was thoroughly convinced that his disability was permanent.

. . . When you tell your child to do anything, and he stops to inquire why, it is advisable to kindly but firmly fetch him a rap across the ear to inform him "that's why!" He will soon get in the way of starting, with charming alacrity, at the word of command.

Mark Twain

ABOUT FATHERS.

When fathers jump up and they holler,
   "Here, Jim! you rascal, you scamp!"
And hustle you round by the collar,
   And waggle their canes and stamp,
You can laugh right out at the riot—
   They like to be sassed and dared;
But when they say, "James," real quiet—
   Oo—oo—that's the time to be scared!

Juliet Wilbor Tompkins

MY FATHER

Because of him I cannot say this world
Is weary, or a failure, or a fraud,
Or that a lovely vessel must be flawed,
Or that the hopeful mind is not as brave
As any splendid action that we laud.

Because of him I cannot say the fall
Is sad, or that the winter is too hard,
Or that the spring by transiency is marred,
Or that the summer in its natural fields
Already by the coming frost is scarred.

Because of him whose mind is more my sire
Than body, and whose heart has been my grace,
I cannot say that man, whom years efface,
Is not the strong effacer in the end
Of all that's selfish, trivial, and base.

—*Virginia Moore*

ONLY A DAD

Only a dad with a tired face,
Coming home from the daily race,
Bringing a little of gold or fame
To show how well he has played the game,
And glad in his heart that his own rejoice
To see him come and to hear his voice.

Only a dad with a brood of four,
One of ten million men or more,
Plodding along in the daily strife
Bearing the whips and scorns of life
With never a whimper of pain or hate,
For the sake of those who at home await.

Only a dad neither rich nor proud,
Merely one of a surging crowd,
Toiling, striving, from day to day,
Facing whatever may come his way.
Silent whenever his own condemn,
Braving it all for the love of them.

Only a dad, but he gives his all
To smooth the way for his children small,
Doing with courage stern and grim
The deeds that his father did for him.
He's only a dad, but does his best.
Make him your pal, he'll do the rest!

Anonymous

Independence Day

Independence Day, or The Fourth of July as it is more commonly called, is the anniversary of the adoption of the Declaration of Independence by the Continental Congress on July 4, 1776. It is the greatest American holiday, as it commemorates the birth of the United States as a nation. It is observed as a legal holiday in every state and territory of the United States and is celebrated by Americans everywhere.

Independence and separation from Great Britain were not at first thought of by the American colonies, and it was some time before the idea became general. Very early in the conflict, Samuel Adams and some of the more ardent patriots advocated a union of the colonies and the formation of an independent government. The majority of Americans, however, hoped for reconciliation and believed that in time the grievances of the colonists would be remedied. But it finally became evident that it would be impossible to come to any understanding with the King of England, and the sentiment in favor of independence grew stronger.

The Continental Congress, on May 15, 1776, adopted a resolution recommending all the colonies to form for themselves independent governments and declaring that the American people could no longer conscientiously support any government deriving its authority from the King of England since the King had withdrawn his protection from the inhabitants of the United Colonies.

On Friday, June 7, 1776, Richard Henry Lee of Virginia introduced into Congress the following resolution: "Resolved, That these United Colonies are, and of right ought to be, free and independent States, that they are absolved from all allegiance to the British Crown, and that all political connection between them and the State of Great Britain is, and ought to be, totally dissolved."

This resolution was at once seconded by John Adams of Massachusetts, but after much discussion it was found that the delegates from some of the colonies were not prepared for an immediate declaration of independence. It was, therefore, decided to postpone action until July 1st so that the other colonies could decide on the question. Most of the colonies promptly declared themselves and by the first of July instructions in favor of independence had been received from all except New York. The Tory party was unusually powerful in New York, and, because of its exposed situation, this colony was likely to suffer more than any other from the war with Great Britain. Opposition to independence was therefore very strong in New York, though the sentiment in its favor was growing rapidly. When July 1st arrived, the matter was still under discussion. and the New York delegates had not received instructions.

At the time set, Congress resumed the consideration of the "resolution regarding independence." John Adams supported it by a powerful speech, and, after some debate, the resolution, as presented by Lee, was adopted, July 2, 1776, twelve of the colonies voting in favor of it. The New York delegates were excused from voting as they had not yet received sufficient instructions. Each colony had one vote in Congress, a majority of the delegates of the colony deciding what that vote should be.

Congress then proceeded to consider the form of declaration which should be adopted. To avoid loss of time a committee had been appointed on June 11th to draw up such a paper. This committee consisted of Thomas Jefferson, John Adams, Benjamin Franklin, Roger Sherman, and Robert R. Livingston. The chairman of the committee was Thomas Jefferson and he was chosen to write the Declaration.

Jefferson first submitted his draft of the Declaration to Adams and Franklin. They made only a few verbal alterations. Jefferson then recopied it and turned it over to the committee. They were so pleased with it that they made no changes whatever, but presented it to Congress as written. The Declaration was debated by Congress for two days, and a number of changes were made. Most of these were merely verbal, but there were two important points which Congress struck out of Jefferson's paper. One of these was a bitter attack on the slave trade, and the other a paragraph in which he charged that the English people had been as unjust and guilty towards America as had the King and Parliament. Finally, toward evening on July 4, 1776, the Declaration of Independence was adopted by the unanimous vote of twelve of the thirteen colonies, the New York delegates still being unable to act. [New York took formal action and adopted the Declaration on July 9, 1776.] The Declaration was immediately signed by John Hancock, President of the Continental Congress, and by Charles Thomson, Secretary.

The Declaration was adopted on July 4th, but at that time was signed only by John Hancock, the President of Congress, and Charles Thomson, the Secretary. A few days later, Congress ordered that the Declaration be engrossed on parchment and "signed by every member of the Congress." This engrossed copy was signed on August 2, 1776.

There were therefore three dates which should be considered as marking the birth of American Independence. These are the 2nd of July, when Lee's resolution of independence was adopted; the 4th of July, when the Declaration was adopted; and August 2nd, when the Declaration was signed. It is somewhat strange that more importance has not been given to the 2nd of July in connection with the adoption of independence. The resolution introduced by Richard Henry Lee which declared our independence and which was the actual legal act of separation from the British government was passed on that day. That was the vital event, and the adoption of the form of declaration was a matter of secondary importance. But by common consent, the great anniversary of the United States of America has been dated from the passage of the Declaration, and thus the Fourth of July is celebrated as the birthday of the nation.

THE AMERICAN REPUBLIC

In the fulness of time, a Republic rose up in the wilderness of America. Thousands of years had passed away before this child of the ages could be born. From whatever there was of good in the systems of former centuries she drew her nourishment; the wrecks of the past were her warnings. With the deepest sentiment of faith fixed in her inmost nature, she disenthralled religion from bondage to temporal power, that her worship might be worship only in spirt and in truth.

The wisdom which had passed from India through Greece, with what Greece had added of her own; the jurisprudence of Rome; the Medieval municipalities; the Teutonic method of representation, the political experience of England, the benignant wisdom of the expositors of the law of nature and of nations in France and Holland, all shed on her their selectest influence. She washed the gold of political wisdom from the sands wherever it was found; she cleft it from the rocks; she gleaned it among ruins. Out of all the discoveries of statesmen and sages, out of all the experience of past human life, she compiled a perennial political philosophy, the primordial principles of national ethics.

The wise men of Europe sought the best government in a mixture of monarchy, aristocracy, and democracy; and America went behind these names to extract from them the vital elements of social forms, and blend them harmoniously in the free Commonwealth, which comes nearest to the illustration of the natural equality of all men. She entrusted the guardianship of established rights to law; the movements of reform to the spirit of the people, and drew her force from the happy reconciliation of both.

George Bancroft.

THE DECLARATION
OF INDEPENDENCE

The Declaration of Independence! The interest which in that paper has survived the occasion upon which it was issued, the interest which is of every age and every clime, the interest which quickens with the lapse of years, spreads as it grows old, and brightens as it recedes, is in the principles which it proclaims. It was the first solemn declaration by a nation of the only legitimate foundation of civil government.
It was the corner-stone of a new fabric, destined to cover the surface of the globe. It demolished at a stroke the lawfulness of all governments founded upon conquest. It swept away all the rubbish of accumulated centuries of servitude. It announced in practical form to the world the transcendent truth of the inalienable sovereignty of the people. It proved that the social compact was no figment of the imagination, but a real, solid, and sacred bond of the social union.

John Quincy Adams.

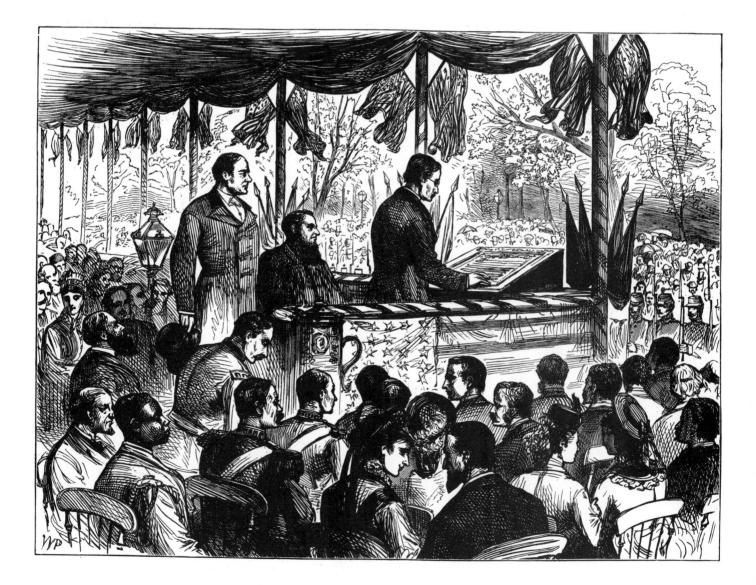

AMERICA

My country, 'tis of thee,
Sweet land of liberty,
   Of thee I sing;
Land where my fathers died,
Land of the pilgrims' pride,
From every mountain-side
   Let Freedom ring.

My native country, thee,
Land of the noble free,—
   Thy name I love;
I love thy rocks and rills,
Thy woods and templed hills;
My heart with rapture thrills
   Like that above.

Let music swell the breeze,
And ring from all the trees,
   Sweet Freedom's song;
Let mortal tongues awake,
Let all that breathe partake,
Let rocks their silence break,—
   The sound prolong.

Our fathers' God, to Thee,
Author of liberty,
   To Thee we sing;
Long may our land be bright
With Freedom's holy light;
Protect us by Thy might,
   Great God, our King.

Samuel Francis Smith

HOROLOGE OF LIBERTY

The world heard: the battle of Lexington—one;
the Declaration of Independence—two;
the surrender of Burgoyne—three;
the siege of Yorktown—four;
the treaty of Paris—five;
the inauguration of Washington—six;
and then it was the sunrise of a new day,
of which we have seen yet only
the glorious forenoon.

Anonymous

THE NATION'S BIRTHDAY

Ring out the joy bells! Once again.
    With waving flags and rolling drums,
We greet the Nation's Birthday, when
    In glorious majesty, it comes.
Ah, day of days! Alone it stands,
    While, like a halo round it cast,
The radiant work of patriot hands,
    Shines the bright record of the past.

Among the nations of the earth,
    What land hath story like our own?
No thought of conquest marked her birth;
    No greed of power e'er was shown
By those who crossed the ocean wild,
    That they might plant upon her sod
A home for Peace and Virtue mild
    And altars rear to Freedom's God.

Mary E. Vandyne

YOUNG AMERICA

Fourth of July, they say, sir,
Is Independence Day, sir,
But really I am certain that there must be some mistake,
For people say, "Be quiet!"
And "I won't have such riot!"
At every teeny-weeny noise that I may chance to make.

Why, when my gun exploded
(I thought it wasn't loaded),
My mother said, "You naughty boy, now stop that fearful noise."
And then our cannon-crackers
(And my! but they *were* whackers!)
Made Grandma say, "Oh, mercy me! you *mustn't* do that, boys!"

"You're much too young to handle
A bomb or Roman candle,"
They always say when I get near to where the fireworks are;
And for a little rocket
I put in Bobby's pocket
My father just now set me down inside the "family jar."

The caution and the warning
Begin at early morning:
It's "Don't do this!" and "Don't do that!" and so, unless I may
Choose my own celebration
For the birthday of our nation,
I don't see why I ought to call it *Independence Day!*

Carolyn Wells

INDEPENDENCE BELL
JULY 4, 1776

There was tumult in the city,
In the quaint old Quaker town,
And the streets were thronged with people
Passing restless up and down—
People gathering at the corners,
Where they whispered lip to ear,
While the sweat stood on their temples,
With the stress of hope and fear.

As the black Atlantic currents
Lash the wild Newfoundland shore,
So they beat about the State House,
So they surged against the door;
And the mingling of their voices
Swelled in harmony profound,
Till the quiet street of Chestnut
Was all turbulent with sound.

Far aloft in the high steeple
  Sat the bellman, old and gray;
He was weary of the tyrant
  And his iron-sceptred sway.
So he sat with one hand ready
  On the clapper of the bell,
Till his eye should catch the signal,
  The expected news to tell.

See! See! the dense crowd quivers
  As beside the door a boy
Looks forth with hands uplifted,
  His eyes alight with joy.
Hushed the people's swelling murmur
  As they listen breathlessly—
"Ring!" he shouts; "ring, grandpapa!
  Ring! oh, ring for liberty!"

Quickly at the welcome signal
  The old bellman lifts his hand;
Forth he sends the good news, making
  Iron music through the land.
How they shouted! What rejoicing!
  How the old bell shook the air,
Till the clang of freedom echoed
  From the belfries everywhere.

The old State House bell is silent,
  Hushed is now its clamorous tongue,
But the spirit it awakened
  Still is living, ever young.
And we'll ne'er forget the bellman
  Who, that great day in July,
Hailed the birth of Independence,
  Which, please God, shall never die.

Unknown

THE BIRTHDAY OF THE NATION

This is that day of the year which announced to mankind the great fact of American Independence! This fresh and brilliant morning blesses our vision with another beholding of the birthday of our Nation; and we see that Nation, of recent origin, now among the most considerable and powerful, and spreading from sea to sea over the continent.

On the Fourth Day of July, 1776, the representatives of the United States of America, in Congress assembled, declared that these Colonies are, and ought to be, free and independent States. This declaration, made by most patriotic and resolute men, trusting in the justice of their cause and the protection of Heaven,—and yet not without deep solicitude and anxiety,—has now stood for seventy-five years. It was sealed in blood. It has met dangers and overcome them. It has had detractors, and abashed them all. It has had enemies, and conquered them. It has had doubting friends, but it has cleared all doubts away; and now, to-day, raising its august form higher than the clouds, twenty millions of people contemplate it with hallowed love, and the world beholds it, and the consequences that have followed from it, with profound admiration.

This anniversary animates and gladdens all American hearts. On other days of the year we may be party men,
indulging in controversies more or less important to the public good.
We may have likes and dislikes, and we may maintain our political differences,
often with warm, and sometimes with angry feelings.
But to-day we are Americans all; and all, nothing but Americans.
As the great luminary over our heads, dissipating foes and mist, now cheers the whole atmosphere,
so do the associations connected with this day disperse all sullen and cloudy weather
in the minds and feelings of true Americans. Every man's heart swells within him.
Every man's port and bearing becomes
somewhat more proud and lofty as he remembers that seventy-five years have rolled away, and that the
great inheritance of Liberty is still his,—his, undiminished and unimpaired; his, in all its original glory;
his to enjoy, his to protect, his to transmit to future generations.

Daniel Webster

JES' PLAIN TORPEDOES

The good old Fourth's a-comin'—the best day in the year,
And little chaps get anxious-like, when once it's drawin' near;
They talk of firecrackers and they dream about the noise,
The dear old Fourth was certainly jes' made fer little boys.
Bill's got a great big cannon, with fuse you have to light,
And lots of great big crackers that's filled with dynamite;
But I'm a little feller—ain't half as old as he,
And I guess that plain torpedoes will have to do fer me!

Pa says giant crackers ain't fit fer little chaps,
He's sore on all toy pistols and hates those paper caps,
He don't intend his children shall ever celebrate
By blowing off their fingers—he says they'll have to wait.
"You're nothin' but a baby," my father says, "as yet,
And your daddy can't quite spare you; he needs you bad, you bet.
Bill's got some giant crackers? Well, that I know is true,
But I guess that plain torpedoes will have to do fer you."

It's hard to have big brothers, and watch them at their play,
And jes' to be a little chap and sort o' in the way;
To have folks always tell you, you can't do thus and so,
Because you're jes' a little chap—not old enough, you know.
But ma, she sees I'm tearful, so she takes me in her lap
And says: "Why, what's the matter, you're cryin', little chap."
Then, as she bends to kiss me, I'm brave as I can be;
I guess that plain torpedoes are good enough fer me!

Louis E. Thayer

AFTER THE FOURTH OF JULY

We put him to bed in his little nightgown,
The most battered youngster there was in the town;
Yet he said as he opened his only well eye,
"Rah, rah, for the jolly old Fourth of July!"

Two thumbs and eight fingers with lint were tied up,
On his head was a bump like an upside-down cup,
And his smile was distorted and his nose all awry,
From the glorious Fourth of July.

We were glad; he had started abroad with the sun,
All the day had lived in the powder and fun;
While the boom of the cannon roared up to the sky,
To salute Young America's Fourth of July!

I said we were glad all the pieces were there,
As we plastered and bound them with tenderest care,
But out of the wreck came the words, with a sign,
"If to-morrow was only the Fourth of July!"

He will grow all together again, never fear,
And be ready to celebrate freedom next year;
Meanwhile all his friends are most thankful there lies
A crackerless twelvemonth 'twixt Fourth of Julys.

We kissed him good-night on his powder-specked face,
We laid his bruised hands softly down in their place,
And he murmured, as sleep closed his one open eye,
"I wish every day was the Fourth of July."

M. Phelps Dawson

Labor Day

The dignity of labor was a major theme of the nineteenth century, growing in intensity as the first stirrings of a united labor movement grew out of the Industrial Revolution. Although, as even recent history shows us, the recognition of the worker as more than a "machine" with muscles has been a slow and even bloody struggle, nineteenth-century writers tended to romanticize work and its inherent dignity. The following passage, by a writer whose name is long lost in history, is typical:

"By *hammer and hand all arts do stand* was the ancient motto of mechanics' guilds or associations. In the hammer lies the wealth of a nation. Its metalic clink points out the abode of industry and labor. By it are alike forged the glittering sword of contention and the dusty plowshare of agriculture, the ponderous engines that almost shake the world, and the tiny needle which unites alike the costly silks and satins of a queen and the rough homespun of the laborer.

"Not a house is built, not a ship floats, not a carriage rolls, not a wheel spins, not an engine thunders, not a press speaks, not a bugle peals, not a spade delves, not a banner floats, without having endured the blows of the hammer. The hammer teaches us that great ends and large results can be accomplished only by good, hard, vigorous blows; that, if we would attain usefulness, and reach the full perfection of what we are capable of becoming, we must not shrink from the hardships, buffetings, and hard knocks of life, but only learn to cultivate the power of patient endurance."

It is not known just when or where the idea of having a holiday devoted to the cause of labor originated. The credit of first putting the idea into execution, however, appears to belong to Peter J. McGuire, the Secretary of the Central Labor Union of New York City. In 1882 he corresponded with various other labor organizations in the state about the matter, and on Tuesday, September 5th, a great parade of labor organizations was held in New York City.

The next year another great labor parade was held on the first Monday in September. In 1884, at the suggestion of George R. Lloyd, of the Knights of Labor, it was decided that all future labor parades should be held on the first Monday in September.

These celebrations were so successful that the idea was taken up by the labor organizations in other states and agitation was started to induce the legislatures of the various states to declare this day a legal holiday. The matter was taken up by the National Labor Federation, and before long the first Monday in September was made a legal holiday in most of the states.

Oregon was the first to take action, and on February 21, 1887, Labor Day was declared a legal holiday in the state. This was followed by Colorado, New Jersey, New York, and

Massachusetts in the same year; Connecticut, Nebraska, and Pennsylvania in 1889; Iowa and Ohio in 1890; and within a few years most of the other states had taken similar action. It is now a legal holiday in every state and territory in the Union.

In 1894 Congress passed a law designating the first Monday in September a public holiday. In this act the day is defined as "the day celebrated and known as Labor's Holiday." Of course, this law made Labor Day a legal holiday only in the District of Columbia and in the Federal offices throughout the country. Congress has no authority to create a holiday in any of the states, but this official recognition of Labor Day strongly influenced the state legislatures, and it was not long before those states which had not already recognized the day took the necessary steps to make it a legal holiday.

The celebration of Labor Day in its formative years was marked by great parades, but these were long ago abandoned. The holiday is now principally observed as a three-day weekend, the final extended holiday of the summer, and, in fact, as the traditional "end" of summer. As a result, some people believe that the day has lost its "meaning." But, in a very real sense, they are mistaken, for Peter J. McGuire himself chose the date on seasonal grounds and without any association with historical events in mind. "I suggested the first Monday in September of every year for such a holiday," he wrote, "as it would come at the most pleasant season of the year, nearly midway between the Fourth of July and Thanksgiving and would fill a wide gap in the chronology of legal holidays." McGuire created Labor Day so that one day in the year could be set aside especially to honor labor. "There were other worthy holidays representative of the religious, civil, and military spirit, but none representative of the industrial spirit—the great vital force of every nation." And what better way to honor labor than by observing a day of rest? As the Bible tells us, even God, at the end of Creation, "rested . . . from all his work."

The essence of Labor Day is perhaps best captured in one of Walt Whitman's most quintessentially American poems:

I hear America singing, the varied carols I hear,
Those of mechanics, each one singing his as it should be blithe and strong.
The carpenter singing his as he measures his plank or beam,
The mason singing his as he makes ready for work or leaves off work,
The boatman singing what belongs to him in his boat,
   the deck-hand singing on the steamboat deck,
The shoemaker singing as he sits on his bench, the hatter singing as he stands.
The wood-cutter's song, the ploughboy's on his way in the morning,
   or at noon intermission or at sundown,
The delicious singing of the mother, or of the young wife at work. . . .

THE DIGNITY
OF LABOR

There is dignity in toil; in toil of the hand as well as toil of the head; in toil to provide for the bodily wants of an individual life, as well as in toil to promote some enterprise of world-wide fame. All labor that tends to supply man's wants, to increase man's happiness, in a word, all labor that is honest, is honorable too.

The Dignity of Labor! Consider its achievements. Dismayed by no difficulty, shrinking from no exertion, exhausted by no struggle, "clamorous Labor knocks with its hundred hands at the golden gate of the morning," obtaining each day, through succeeding centuries, fresh benefactions for the world.

Labor clears the forest, and drains the morass, and makes the wilderness rejoice and blossom as the rose. Labor drives the plow, and scatters the seeds, and reaps the harvest, and grinds the corn, and converts it into bread, the staff of life. Labor gathers the gossamer web of the caterpillar, the cotton from the field, and the fleece from the flock, and weaves them into raiment, soft, and warm, and beautiful—the purple robe of the prince and the gray gown of the peasant being alike its handiwork. Labor molds the brick, and splits the slate, and quarries the stone, and shapes the column, and rears not only the humble cottage, but the gorgeous palace, and the tapering spire, and the stately dome.

Labor, diving deep into the solid earth, brings up its long-hidden stores of coal, to feed ten thousand furnaces, and in millions of habitations to defy the winter's cold. Labor explores the rich veins of deeply-buried rocks, extracting the gold, the silver, the copper, and the tin. Labor smelts the iron, and molds it into a thousand shapes for use and ornament. Labor cuts down the gnarled oak, and hews the timber and builds the ship, and guides it over the deep, bearing to our shores the produce of every clime.

Labor, laughing at difficulties, spans majestic rivers, carries viaducts over marshy swamps, suspends bridges over deep ravines, pierces the solid mountains, with its dark tunnel, blasting rocks, filling hollows, and linking together with its iron but loving grasp all nations of the earth.

Labor, a mighty magician, walks forth into a region uninhabited and waste; he looks earnestly at the scene, so quiet in its desolation; then waving his wonder-working wand, those dreary valleys smile with golden harvests; those barren mountain slopes are clothed with foliage; the furnace blazes; the anvil rings; the busy wheel whirls round; the town appears; the mart of commerce, the hall of science, the temple of religion, rear high their lofty fronts; a forest of masts, gay with varied pennons, rises from the harbor. Science enlists the elements of earth and heaven in its service; Art, awakening, clothes its strength with beauty; Civilization smiles; Liberty is glad; Humanity rejoices; Piety exults; for the voice of industry and gladness is heard on every side.

"Work for some good, be it ever so slowly;
Work for some hope, be it ever so lowly;
Work! for all labor is noble and holy!"

Newman Hall

AMERICAN LABOR

Labor is one of the great elements of society—the great substantial interest on which we all stand. Not feudal service, or predial toil, or the irksome drudgery by one race of mankind subjected to another, but labor, intelligent, manly, independent, thinking and acting for itself, earning its own wages, accumulating those wages into capital, educating childhood, maintaining worship, claiming the right of elective franchise, and helping to uphold the great fabric of the State. That is American labor, and all my sympathies are with it, and my voice, till I am dumb, will be for it.

Daniel Webster.

LABOR SONG

Ah! little they know of true happiness, they whom satiety fills,
Who, flung on the rich breast of luxury, eat of the rankness that kills,
Ah! little they know of the blessedness toil-purchased slumber enjoys
Who, stretched on the hard rack of indolence, taste of the sleep that destroys;
Nothing to hope for, or labor for; nothing to sigh for, or gain;
Nothing to light in its vividness, lightning-like, bosom and brain;
Nothing to break life's monotony, rippling it o'er with its breath;—
Nothing but dulness and lethargy, weariness, sorrow, and death!

But blessed that child of humanity, happiest man among men,
Who, with hammer or chisel or pencil, with rudder or ploughshare or pen,
Laboreth ever and ever with hope through the morning of life,
Winning home and its darling divinities,—love-worshipped children and wife.
Round swings the hammer of industry, quickly the sharp chisel rings,
And the heart of the toiler has throbbings that stir not the bosom of kings,—
He the true ruler and conqueror, he the true king of his race,
Who nerveth his arm for life's combat, and looks the strong world in the face.

Denis Florence MacCarthy

LABOR AND
ITS REWARDS

Labor, indeed, if we would but perceive it, is one of the greatest of earthly blessings. It rewards with health, contentment of mind, cheerfulness of spirit and sound, refreshing sleep; few of which blessings of life are long enjoyed by those who do not daily, in one form or another, labor. And why is this? Because to labor is to perform the business of life; to carry out the purpose for which every human being is called into existence.

Anonymous

THE SOWER'S SONG

Now hands to seed-sheet, boys!
　　We step and we cast; old Time's on wing;
And would ye partake of Harvest's joys,
　　The corn must be sown in spring.
　　　　Fall gently and still, good corn,
　　　　　Lie warm in thy earthy bed;
　　　　And stand so yellow some morn,
　　　　　For beast and man must be fed.

Old earth is a pleasure to see
　　In sunshiny cloak of red and green;
The furrow lies fresh, this year will be
　　As years that are past have been.
　　　　Fall gently and still, good corn,
　　　　　Lie warm in thy earthy bed;
　　　　And stand so yellow some morn,
　　　　　For beast and man must be fed.

Old earth, receive this corn,
　　The son of six thousand golden sires;
All these on thy kindly breast were born;
　　One more thy poor child requires.
　　　　Fall gently and still, good corn,
　　　　　Lie warm in thy earthy bed;
　　　　And stand so yellow some morn,
　　　　　For beast and man must be fed.

Now steady and sure again,
　　And measure of stroke and step we keep;
Thus up and down we cast our grain;
　　Sow well and you gladly reap.
　　　　Fall gently and still, good corn,
　　　　　Lie warm in thy earthy bed;
　　　　And stand so yellow some morn,
　　　　　For beast and man must be fed.

Thomas Carlyle

WORK

The comforter of sorrow and of care;
    The shortener of way prolonged and rude;
The lightener of burden hard to bear;
    The best companion 'mid the solitude;
The draft that soothes the mind and calms the brain;
    The miracle that lifts despair's thick murk;
When other friends would solace bring, in vain,
    Thank God for work!

That boon for which the prince in splendor sighs
    But which attends the humble peasant's lot:
Without which, castles but as prisons rise,
    And with which, prisons crush but strangle not.
The sum of life; all evil's sovereign cure;
    The measure of employer as of clerk;
The true nobility's investiture—
    Thank God for work!

Edwin L. Sabin

Bookbinder

Brewer

Butcher

Carpenter

Cook

Draftsman

Painter

Pharmacist (Red-Blue)

Plumber

Potter

Printer

Saddler

EARTH'S NOBLEMEN

The noblest men I know on earth,
   Are men whose hands are brown with toil,
Who, backed by no ancestral graves,
   Hew down the woods, and till the soil,
And win thereby a prouder name
Than follows kings' or warriors' fame.

The working men, whate'er their task,
   Who carve the stone or bear the hod,
They bear upon their honest brows
   The royal stamp and seal of God;
And worthier are their drops of sweat
Than diamonds in a coronet.

God bless the noble working men,
   Who near the cities of the plain;
Who dig the mines, who build the ships,
   And drive the commerce of the main:
God bless them! for their toiling hands
Have wrought the glory of all lands.

Anonymous

Columbus Day

Christopher Columbus was born in Genoa, Italy, about the year 1446, the exact date being uncertain. His father was a wool comber. From earliest boyhood, Columbus showed great fondness for the sea and spent all his spare time talking with the sailors about their voyages. He studied mathematics, astronomy, and navigation. After leaving school, he worked at his father's trade for a few months, but, when about fourteen years old, he went to sea.

In 1470 Columbus settled in Lisbon, Portugal, and married the daughter of an Italian navigator. While in Lisbon, he supported himself and his family by making maps and charts, and while thus employed, he conceived the idea that India, and the other countries of the East, could be reached by sailing westward.

Long before the beginning of the Christian era, Aristotle, the famous Greek philosopher, had shown that the earth was a round ball. Nearly all the scholars who wrote after him adopted this view, but the people generally believed that the earth was a flat plane surface. If the earth were really a globe, however, it should be possible, by sailing westward across the Atlantic Ocean, to reach the eastern shore of Asia. Soon after 1471 this idea occurred to several men. One of these was Columbus, and he resolved to make the attempt. The object was to reach the rich lands of India, China, and Japan, and the question was which was the shortest route. The Portuguese explorers were sailing southward in the hope of passing around Africa and reaching India. Columbus believed that it would be shorter to sail westward and go straight to Japan. He sought advice from Toscanelli, the famous astronomer, who assured him that this idea was correct. Little was known of the size of Asia, and it was believed that it extended eastward very near to what is now California.

About 1482 Columbus laid his scheme before John II of Portugal. The King referred the matter to a body of scientists, who decided against it. Taking advantage, however, of a detailed plan obtained from Columbus, the king secretly sent out an expedition to examine the route. Too timid to venture far from land, the pilot soon returned to Lisbon and threw ridicule on the project. Columbus left Lisbon in 1484, taking with him his motherless little boy Diego. He presented his idea to the authorities of Genoa and Venice, but was only laughed at. Disheartened, he turned his steps toward Spain. Weary and hungry, he stopped one day at a Franciscan convent to beg some bread for his child. The superior of the convent happened to pass at the time and, entering into conversation with Columbus, was at once impressed with his great idea. This man used his influence to obtain an interview with the King of Spain. It was a long time before this could be done, and in the meantime Columbus offered his idea to other countries without success. Finally he obtained an interview with King Ferdinand and Queen Isabella of Spain and told them of the great plan. But the King and his courtiers laughed at the scheme, and Columbus went away discouraged. Queen Isabella, however, sent for Columbus and offered to pledge her jewels to raise the money to fit out an expedition.

Three very small vessels were made ready for the great voyage. The largest of them was named the *Santa Maria* and was the flagship of Columbus. This was the only ship of the three having a deck covering the entire hold of the vessel. Great difficulty was found in obtaining a crew. The sailors feared to undertake such a voyage, and it was necessary to procure an order from the king to compel them to go. Finally, 120 men were obtained to man the vessels, and on August 3, 1492, Columbus sailed from the port of Palos, Spain. He stopped at the Canary Islands for about a month to refit and repair his ships and on the 6th of September started on his voyage into the unknown seas.

After sailing westward day after day without sight of land, the sailors became frightened and begged Columbus to turn back. When he refused, they became angry, and, declaring that he was mad, threatened to throw him overboard. Columbus, however, suppressed this mutiny and, sternly ordering them back to their work, declared he would not give up the voyage no matter what happened. The very next day unmistakable signs of land appeared, and, at ten at night, Columbus saw a light which looked like a moving torch. Finally, at two o'clock in the morning of October 12, 1492, after a voyage of thirty-five days, land was discovered. This was one of the Bahama Islands, but which one is not known. Here he landed and named the island San Salvador. After discovering several other islands of the West Indies, including Cuba and Haiti, Columbus set sail for Spain and arrived there on March 15, 1493.

In September, 1493, Columbus sailed on his second voyage with 17 ships and 1,500 men. He had difficulty in restraining people from embarking with him, for everyone expected to become rich in the new lands. A colony was settled on the island of Haiti, or Hispaniola as it was then called, but no gold or precious stones were found; instead, the colonists had to endure hardships, sickness, and hunger. The disappointed settlers blamed Columbus, and as the enterprise was a heavy expense on the treasury and brought little in return, he soon lost favor at court. During this voyage he discovered Jamaica and other islands, and returned home in 1496. Two years later he set out on a third voyage. This time steering more to the south, he discovered land which we know to have been South America and sailed along the coast from the mouth of the Orinoco River westward for some distance. Columbus believed this to be Asia and could not understand why he did not find any of Asia's riches. After these discoveries, he sailed to Haiti where he found everything in disorder. The king had again been influenced against him; an officer named Bobadilla had been appointed to supersede Columbus as governor, and he sent Columbus home in chains. This treatment excited the indignation of the Spanish people to such a degree that King Ferdinand professed that it had been done without his sanction. But all Columbus's efforts to obtain redress from the king were unsuccessful.

He was not discouraged, however, and on May 9, 1502, with four vessels and 150 men, Columbus set out on his fourth voyage hoping to find a strait leading into the Indian Ocean from the Caribbean Sea. He explored the coast of Central America, but of course failed to find any such passage, and after many difficulties and disasters and having added nothing to his former discoveries, he returned to Spain in November, 1504. Queen Isabella was dead, King Ferdinand proved ungrateful, and Columbus died poor and broken-hearted, at Valladolid, Spain, May 20, 1506. Columbus died thinking he had found a short route to Asia and never knew that he had discovered a new continent.

THE DISCOVERY OF AMERICA

It was on Friday morning, the 21st of October, 1492, that Columbus first beheld the New World. On landing, he threw himself on his knees, kissed the earth, and returned thanks to God with tears of joy. His example was followed by the rest, whose hearts indeed overflowed with the same feelings of gratitude.

Columbus then, rising, drew his sword, displayed the royal standard, and took solemn possession in the name of the Castilian sovereigns, giving the island the name of San Salvador. Having complied with the requisite forms and ceremonies, he called upon all present to take the oath of obedience to him, as admiral and viceroy representing the persons of the sovereigns.

The feelings of the crew now burst forth in the most extravagant transports. They thronged about the Admiral with overflowing zeal, some embracing him, others kissing his hands. Those who had been most mutinous and turbulent during the voyage were now most devoted and enthusiastic. Some begged favors of him, as if he had already wealth and honors in his gift. Many abject spirits, who had outraged him by their insolence, now crouched at his feet, begging pardon for all the trouble they had caused him, and promising the blindest obedience for the future.

Washington Irving

COLUMBUS

Behind him lay the gray Azores,
   Behind the Gates of Hercules;
Before him not the ghost of shores,
   Before him only shoreless seas.
The good mate said: "Now must we pray,
   For lo! the very stars are gone.
Brave Admiral, speak, what shall I say?"
   "Why, say, 'Sail on! sail on! and on!' "

"My men grow mutinous day by day;
   My men grow ghastly, wan, and weak."
The stout mate thought of home; a spray
   Of salt wave washed his swarthy cheek.
"What shall I say, brave Admiral, say,
   If we sight naught but seas at dawn?"
"Why, you shall say at break of day,
   'Sail on! sail on! sail on! and on!' "

They sailed and sailed, as winds might blow,
   Until at last the blanched mate said:
"Why, now not even God would know
   Should I and all my men fall dead.
These very winds forget their way,
   For God from these dread seas is gone.
Now speak, brave Admiral, speak and say"—
   He said: "Sail on! sail on! and on!"

They sailed. They sailed. Then spake the mate:
   "This mad sea shows his teeth to-night.
He curls his lip, he lies in wait,
   He lifts his teeth, as if to bite!
Brave Admiral, say but one good word:
   What shall we do when hope is gone?"
The words leapt like a leaping sword:
   "Sail on! sail on! sail on! and on!"

Then, pale and worn, he paced his deck,
   And peered through darkness. Ah, that night
Of all dark nights! And then a speck—
   A light! a light! at last! a light!
It grew, a starlit flag unfurled!
   It grew to be Time's burst of dawn.
He gained a world; he gave that world
   Its grandest lesson: "On! sail on!"

Joaquin Miller

THE *NIÑA*, THE *PINTA*, AND THE *SANTA MARIA*

Only the *Santa Maria* was a *Nao* or full-rigged ship, after the fashion of a galleon, with a complete deck: the two others, the fast-sailing *Pinta,* the "Painted Lady," and the little *Niña,* the "Baby," were light vessels with three masts, open amidships and decked at bow and stern, rising to a considerable height, castellated fore and aft, and with cabins for the crew. The Niña had only lateen sails. The *Santa Maria* was chartered on behalf of the Queen and carried the Admiral's flags. Columbus himself commanded her. The captain of the *Pinta* was Martin Alonzo Pinzon, and his brother Vincente Yanez commanded the *Niña.* Sancho Ruiz, Pedro Alonzon Nino, and Francisco Roldan (the subsequent rebel) were engaged as pilots. Rodrigo de Escobar accompanied the exposition as Royal Notary: Diego de Arana of Cordova, uncle of Beatrice, was Chief Alguazil, and Rodrigo Sanchez of Segovia was Inspector-General and representative of the Government. The owner of the *Santa Maria,* who was later to become famous as the cartographer, Juan de la Cosa, served on his own ship as *maestro,* and the owner of the *Pinta* seems to have taken part in the expedition as passenger. A few other persons accompanied it in the roles of what might be called private adventurers. One doctor and a surgeon were found prepared to undertake the dangerous voyage.

Jacob Wasserman
from *Columbus: Don Quixote of the Seas*

COLUMBUS

Give me white paper!
This which you use is black and rough with smears
Of sweat and grime, and fraud, and blood and tears,
Crossed with the story of men's sins and fears,
Of battle and of famine all these years,
　　When all God's children had forgot their birth,
　　And drudged and fought and died like beasts of earth.

"Give me white paper!"
One storm-trained seaman listened to the word;
What no man saw he saw, he heard what no man heard.
　　In answer he compelled the sea
　　To eager man to tell
　　The secret she had kept so well!
Left blood and guilt and tyranny behind,—
Sailing still West the hidden shore to find;
　　For all mankind that unstained scroll unfurled,
　　Where God might write anew the story of the World.

Edward Everett Hale

THE RETURN OF COLUMBUS

In the spring of 1493, while the court was still at Barcelona, letters were received from Christopher Columbus, announcing his return to Spain and the successful achievement of his great enterprise, by the discovery of land beyond the western ocean. The delight and astonishment, raised by this intelligence were proportioned to the skepticism with which his project had been originally viewed. The sovereigns were now filled with a natural impatience to ascertain the extent and particulars of the important discovery; and they transmitted instant instructions to the Admiral to repair to Barcelona as soon as he should have made the preliminary arrangements for the further prosecution of his enterprise.

It was the middle of April before Columbus reached Barcelona. The nobility and cavaliers in attendance on the court, together with the authorities of the city, came to the gates to receive him, and escorted him to the royal presence. Ferdinand and Isabella were seated, with their son, Prince John, under a superb canopy of state, awaiting his arrival. On his approach they rose from their seats, and, extending their hands to him to salute, caused him to be seated before them. These were unprecedented marks of condescension to a person of Columbus's rank, in the haughty and ceremonious court of Castile.

It was, indeed, the proudest moment in the life of Columbus. He had fully established the truth of his long-contested theory, in the face of argument, sophistry, sneers, skepticism, and contempt. He had achieved this not by chance, but by calculation, supported through the most adverse circumstances by consummate conduct. The honors paid him, which had hitherto been reserved only for rank, or fortune, or military success, purchased by the blood and tears of thousands, were, in his case, a homage to intellectual power, successfully exerted in behalf of the noblest interests of humanity.

William H. Prescott.

A BOY'S ESSAY ON "COLUMBUS"

"Columbus was a man who could make an egg stand on end without breaking it. The king of Spain said to Columbus: 'Can you discover America?' 'Yes,' said Columbus, 'if you will give me a ship.' So he had a ship and sailed over the sea in the direction where he thought America ought to be found. The sailors quarreled and said they believed there was no such place. But after many days the pilot came to him and said: 'Columbus, I see land.' 'Then that is America,' said Columbus. When the ship came near, the land was full of red men. Columbus said: 'Is this America?' 'Yes, it is,' said they. Then he said: 'I suppose you are the Indians?' 'Yes,' they said, 'we are.' The chief said: 'I suppose you are Columbus.' 'You are right,' said he. Then the chief turned to his men and said: 'There is no help for it; we are discovered at last.' "

—*London Standard.*

CHRISTOPHER C——.

In the city of Genoa, over the sea,
In a beautiful country called Italy,
There lived a sailor called Christopher C——;
A very wise man for his times was he.

He studied the books and maps and charts,
All that they knew about foreign parts;
And he said to himself; "There certainly oughter
Be some more land to balance the water.

"As sure as a gun the earth is round;
Some day or other a way will be found
To get to the east by sailing west;
Why shouldn't I find it as well as the rest?"

The court philosopher shook his head,
Laughing at all that Christopher said;
But the Queen of Spain said, "Christopher C——
Here is some money; go and see."

That is just what he wanted to do,
And in fourteen hundred and ninety-two,
From the port of Palos one August day
This Christopher C—— went sailing away.

He sailed and sailed with the wind and tide,
But he never supposed that the sea was so wide,
And the sailors grumbled, and growled, and cried:
"We don't believe there's another side.

"Oh take us back to our native shore,
Or we never will see our wives any more.
Take us back, O Christopher C——,
Or we'll tumble you overboard into the sea."

In spite of their threats he wouldn't do it;
There was land ahead, and Christopher knew it;
They found San Salvador, green and low,
And the Captain shouted, "I told you so!

"This is the land King Solomon knew,
Where myrrh, and aloes, and spices grew,
Where gold, and silver, and gems are found,
Plenty as pebbles all over the ground."

They thought they had sailed clear round the ball,
But it wasn't the other side at all,
But an island, laying just off a shore
Nobody had ever seen before.

They planted their flag on a flowery plain,
To show that the country belonged to Spain;
But it never once entered Christopher's mind
That North America lay behind.

Then Christopher C——, he sailed away,
And said he would come another day;
But, if he had stayed here long enough,
We should talk Spanish or some such stuff.

Anonymous

HOW COLUMBUS
FOUND AMERICA

Columbus stood upon the deck;
 "Go home!" the sailors cried;
"Not if I perish on the wreck,"
 Great Christopher replied.

Next day the crew got out their knives
 And went for Captain C.
"Go home," they yelled, "and save our lives."
 "Wait one more day," said he.

"Then if I cannot tell how far
 We're from the nearest land
I'll take you home." "Agreed, we are!"
 Answered the sea-sick band.

That night when all were fast asleep
 Columbus heaved the lead,
And measuring the water deep,
 Took notes and went to bed.

To-morrow dawned. Naught could be seen
 But water, wet and cold,
Columbus, smiling and serene,
 Looked confident and bold.

"Now, Cap! How far from land are we?"
 The mutineers out cried.
"Just ninety fathoms," Captain C.
 Most truthfully replied.

"And if you doubt it, heave the lead
 And measure, same as I."
"You're right," the sailors laughed. "Great head!
 We'll stick to you or die."

And thus, in fourteen ninety-two,
 America was found,
Because the great Columbus knew
 How far off was the ground.

—H. C. Dodge.

Halloween

Until the mid-nineteenth century, Halloween was not generally recognized as being a holiday worthy of celebration in the United States. Even today, of course, it is observed solely as an evening affair and is considered something suitable for children only. An ancient festival day, it has its roots in the most pagan of Roman rites and Druidic customs. Held on the last day of October each year, Halloween derives its name from later Christian associations, and has been stripped of most sinister connotations. Literally the name means the eve or evening before All Hallows Day, November 1st, a time set apart on the Christian calendar for honoring departed souls. Until early in the twentieth century, the holiday was most often spelled "Hallowe'en," a logical abbeviation of Hallow-even.

America's earliest settlers from England, staunch Protestants, did not think much of Druids, the Romans and their gods, or followers of the Roman Catholic faith. Even the traditional Church of England discouraged the practice of praying for departed souls and the ringing of church bells to somehow assist disembodied spirits in their ascent from earthly haunts or purgatory to heavenly spheres. It all smacked of the Devil and his works. This is not to say, however, that the average Protestant settler did not entertain notions considered just as peculiar today as those held by the Catholic. Belief in witchcraft was widespread, and in New England reached a particularly ugly stage in the late seventeenth century. That there were also various kinds of spooks and hobgoblins at work in the world was no doubt a widely held popular notion. It was not, however, until the arrival of immigrants from such a traditionally Roman Catholic area as Ireland that the custom of celebrating Halloween came into any sort of general practice.

The early Irish settler had a well-developed appreciation for the supernatural, and was not at all reluctant to express it in story and symbolic act. It is to the Irish that we owe that most familiar of Hallween icons, the jack-o'-lantern. In legend a stingy drunkard by the name of Jack is said to have been given such a feeble light by the Devil himself after being driven from both heaven and hell. With this strange lantern in hand, Jack still roams the earth in search of a place of rest.

With the loosening of the authority of the minister in nineteenth-century America and Great Britain, there was a revival of particular customs that had not been in vogue since before the English Reformation. All had some basis in Druidic or Celtic tradition, and most were as innocuous as most Halloween activities are today. During the 1800s, these were considerably romanticized and stripped of their more macabre overtones. By the end of the nineteenth century, dressing in a "scary" or strange costume and making the rounds of the neighborhood in search of handouts of apples, nuts, and candies was an annual treat for children. Several hundred years earlier, similarly masked individuals—representing lost souls—marched solemnly through a village with the intention of escorting the ghosts of the departed from town.

Halloween was once the time when the witches would dance with abandon and turn their mean tricks on innocent humans. In Scotland a woman thought to be possessed by the devil turned hag-like this one night of the year and flew up the chimney on a broomstick. Her attendants were sleek black cats. Today these creatures are seen to be made of only crêpe paper or cardboard.

Halloween has thus been rendered harmless to nearly everyone. Only in America has it often become the occasion for reckless behavior and vandalism. Indeed, in America alone during modern times, it has sometimes seemed that the devil and his disciples were at work on All Hallows Eve. Soaping of windows, screens, and cars; the destruction of mail and newspaper boxes; the decorating of the countryside with toilet paper and upsetting trash cans—these practices and others much more serious have led numerous communities to police and sometimes curtail the activities of even the most childlike Halloween revelers. In recent years there has been an attempt to redirect the energy of youngsters toward a more worthwhile cause—the raising of funds for UNICEF. The familiar cry "trick or treat" is now often answered with a financial contribution that will help meet the basic needs of deprived children everywhere in the world.

As worthy as this activity is, it should not be used to paper over the underlying festivity of Halloween. This was a holiday which was enjoyed in places where it was safe to tour the neighborhood in costume in the early evening. It was fun to dress up as a pirate, a witch, a skeleton, the headless horseman. The only distress for most participants came from eating too much of the treats available at each house or apartment. The games of Halloween were enjoyable too—bobbing for apples, paring an apple and attempting to read the first letter of a girl or boy friend's name from the paring. Halloween is usually the last holiday each year that can be enjoyed outdoors before the winter closes in. Around a bonfire, stories of strange happenings take on a magical spell. There *should* be one night for entertaining notions of the supernatural world of the imagination.

HALLOWE'EN

Pixie, kobold, elf, and sprite,
All are on their rounds to-night;
In the wan moon's silver ray,
Thrives their helter-skelter play.

Fond of cellar, barn, or stack,
True unto the almanac,
They present to credulous eyes
Strange hobgoblin mysteries.

Cabbage stumps—straws wet with dew—
Apple-skins, and chestnuts too,
And a mirror for some lass
Show what wonders come to pass.

Doors they move, and gates they hide;
Mischiefs that on moonbeams ride
Are their deeds—and, by their spells,
Love records its oracles.

Don't we all, of long ago,
By the ruddy fireplace glow,
In the kitchen and the hall,
Those queer, autumn pranks recall?

Eery shadows were they then—
But to-night they come again;
Were we once more but sixteen,
Precious would be Hallowe'en.

Joel Benton

HALLOWE'EN HAPPENINGS

For real, rollicking, frolicking fun, there is nothing more jolly than a Hallowee'en party.

The observance of Hallowe'en, or All-Hallow Eve, is a tradition handed down from the ancient Druids, who celebrated their harvest festival on the last day of October. The next day was All-Hallows', or All-Saints' Day, and so they called the festival All-Hallow E'en.

The gay games of modern times are not much like the solemn rites of the Druids, but a connection may be traced between the supernatural beliefs of the ancients, and the burlesque attempts to pry into the mysteries of the future, which our own Hallowe'en fun represents.

Long after the time of the Druids, simple-minded country people continued to believe in charms and witchcraft, and especially claimed that on the night of October 31 witches and goblins held revel, and fairies danced about in the woods. From these spirits, or their manifestations, it was believed that the future could be foretold and human destinies discovered. As our celebration of the occasion is merely a whimsical adaptation of all this, there is one thing clear at the outset: To a successful Hallowe'en party, the young guests must bring a large stock of imagination, a zest for merriment, and an unfailing fund of good humor. For many Hallowe'en tricks result in turning the laugh on one or another, and this must be accepted in a gay, good-natured spirit. Old-fashioned Hallowe'en parties were held in the kitchen, and where this is practicable, it is a good plan for many of the games. But all of the rooms used should be decorated with trophies of the harvest. Pumpkins, apples, grain stalks, and autumn leaves offer materials for beautiful and effective trimming; and, if desired, draperies of red and yellow cheese-cloth, and

ornamentations of red and yellow crêpe paper, may be added. Jack-o'-lanterns are, of course, a necessity. All boys know how to scoop out pumpkins, cut grotesque faces on them and insert candles. But don't stop with the pumpkins. Make lanterns also of queer-shaped squashes, turnips, cucumbers, and even apples.

For invitations to a Hallowe'en party, find a large oak or maple leaf in bright autumn tints. Lay this on a paper and trace the shape, then tint it in gay colors, and write the invitation thereon; or, use cards decorated with tiny sketches of Jack-o'-lanterns, witches on broomsticks or black cats. Some such verse as this may appear on the card:

Hallowe'en will tell you true
What the Future holds for you.
Thursday evening, just at eight,
Come, prepared to learn your Fate.

When the guests arrive, the house should be but dimly lighted, and a weird and mysterious atmosphere should prevail. Red shades on the lights, or a red screen before the open fire, give a soft, rich glow. The guests may be received by some one dressed as a witch, or garbed in a white sheet to represent a ghost. Welcome should be spoken in sepulchral tones and accompanied by groans or wails. Some one may play snatches of wild, weird music on the piano, or strike occasional clanging notes from muffled gongs. Jack-o'-lanterns peer from unexpected places, and, if convenient, an Aeolian harp may be arranged in an open window. The awesomeness of effect will be sufficiently relieved by the irrepressible laughter of the merry guests as they arrive.

It is well to begin with the simpler sort of Hallowe'en games. First comes the Initial Letter. Pare an apple in one continuous piece. Swing it slowly around your head three times, and let it fall on the floor. The letter it forms as it falls will be the initial of your future Fate. This incantation should be pronounced as the experiment is tried:

Paring, paring, long and green,
Tell my Fate for Hallowe'en.

The Mirror is another test. A girl must stand with her back to a mirror, and, looking over her shoulder, repeat this charm:

Mirror, mirror, tell to me
Who my future Fate may be.
Ere the magic moments pass,
Frame his picture in the glass.

A merry trick is Blowing out the Candle. A boy and a girl may try this at the same time. Each must be blindfolded, and after turning around three times may try to blow out a lighted candle. A prize may be given to the one who succeeds. Hallowe'en prizes should be plentiful and of trifling value. Also, let them be, as far as possible, appropriate to the occasion. Pin-cushions may represent tiny pumpkins, tomatoes, apples, or radishes. Peanut owls, black velvet witches, chenille imps, and other weird or grotesque figures will suggest themselves, and in the shops may be found inexpensive trinkets suggestive of the day.

Another prize game is Biting the Apple. A large apple is suspended by a string, and two or more players try to catch it and take a bite. It is not permissible to touch the apple with the hands, and if the merry contestants forget this, their hands may be tied behind their backs.

A good variation of this game is to take a barrel hoop and suspend it from the ceiling so that it will swing and revolve freely. From it, at intervals, suspend by short strings, apples, nuts, candies, cakes, and candle-ends. Who gets by chance a candle-end, must pay a forfeit, while the dainties are considered prizes of themselves. Another rollicking form of this game is called Bobbing for Apples. A large tub is half-filled with water, and in it a number of apples are set floating. Previously, the initials of each one of the guests have been cut upon an apple. All those with girls' initials are put in at one time, and the boys endeavor to draw out the apples with their teeth, while their hands are tied behind them. Then the girls "bob" likewise for the apples which bear the boys' initials. The apple secured is supposed to represent the future Fate of the lad or lassie.

A true Hallowe'en game is the Fateful ice-cream. In a mound or brick of ice-cream are hidden a dime, a

ring, and a thimble. The dish is passed around and each guest eats a spoonful.
Whoever chances to get the dime is destined to great wealth; the ring betokens matrimony, and the thimble
single blessedness for life.
Popping Corn, though of no fateful significance, is an indispensable part of the program, and must not on any account be omitted. Pop-corn, somehow, seems to belong to Hallowe'en.
Popping Chestnuts is a more serious matter. Two chestnuts are laid on an open fire or hot stove, and the inquiring maiden names each for a youth of her acquaintance. According to the Hallowe'en superstition, if one nut pops or bursts, that suitor is the unlucky one, but if it burns with a steady glow until consumed to ashes, it shows a true and faithful lover. So old is this particular ceremony, that no less a poet than John Gay thus writes of it:

Two hazel-nuts I throw into the flame,
And to each nut I give a sweetheart's name,
This, with the loudest bounce me sore amazed;
That, in a flame of brightest color blazed.
As blazed the nut, so may thy passion glow,
For 't was thy nut that did so brightly glow.

Threading the Needle is a test of a steady hand. A boy or a girl may hold a needle while the other tries to thread it. Each must use but one hand, and sometimes he or she is made to hold in the other hand a full cup of water which must not be spilled. If the needle is finally threaded the two are presumably destined for each other. The other young people help or hinder the pair by chanting this charm:

> *Needly, thready,*
> *Steady! Steady!*
> *Where's the thread? The needle's ready.*
> *Now you have it, and now you don't!*
> *Now she will, and now she won't!*
> *Aim it true, and aim it straight,*
> *And behold your future Fate!*

The Game of Who's Got the Ring, though old, is another traditional feature of the occasion. The players stand in a circle, holding hands, while one stands in the middle. A ring is passed swiftly and slyly from one hand to another, and the player inside the circle must try to capture it as it goes. All sing in concert:

> *Ring go round, ring go round!*
> *You can find it, I'll be bound.*
> *Now it's here, and now it's there,*
> *Changing, ranging, everywhere.*
> *Watch more carefully, and then*
> *You may see it!*
> *Fooled again!*

Needless to say, the last line often rings out most appropriately.

The Bowl of Flour is a pretty test of who shall be the first bride or bridegroom of the group. Pack a bowl very tightly with flour, and in it drop a wedding-ring. Invert the bowl on a platter, and remove it carefully, leaving a compact mound of flour. With a broad, silver knife, let each guest cut off a slice of the flour. As it crumbles, if it contain the ring, it is an omen of approaching marriage.

Counting the Seeds is a game all may play at once. Each is given an apple, which is at once cut in two, crossways, and the seeds counted. If two seeds are found, it portends an early marriage; three indicates a legacy; four, great wealth; five, an ocean trip; six, great public fame; seven, the possession of any gift most desired by the finder.

Nutshell Boats make a pretty test of Fortune. In the half shells of English walnuts are fitted masts made of matches, and tiny, paper sails. On each sail is written the name of a guest, and the boats are set afloat in a tub of water. If two glide together, it indicates a similar fate for their owners; if one sails alone, it means a lonely life. A gentle stirring up of the water will make the boats behave in an amusing manner.

The Three Saucers is said to be an unerring revelation of Fate. One saucer must contain clear water, another, soapy water, or water into which a drop of ink has been spilled, and the third saucer is empty. A girl is blindfolded, and must dip her finger into one saucer. If the empty one, she will always remain single; if the soapy water, she will marry a widower; but if she touch the clear water, her Fate will be a handsome and wealthy husband.

And as a parting peep into the mysteries of the Future, let the hostess, or some grown-up read the palms of the young people (Fig. 10). This need not be scientific palmistry, but a merry make-believe, wherein the fortune-teller can gravely assure the young inquirers of astounding events or fabulous delights which may come into their future lives.

Carolyn Wells

HALLOWE'EN

Hark! Hark to the wind! 'Tis the night, they say,
When all souls come back from the far away—
The dead, forgotten this many a day!

And the dead remembered—ay! long and well—
And the little children whose spirits dwell
In God's green garden of asphodel.

Have you reached the country of all content,
O souls we know, since the day you went
From this time-worn world, where your years were spent?

Would you come back to the sun and the rain,
The sweetness, the strife, the thing we call pain,
And then unravel life's tangle again?

I lean to the dark—Hush!—was it a sigh?
Or the painted vine-leaves that rustled by?
Or only a night-bird's echoing cry?

Virna Sheard

THE SPELL

At even o' Hallowmas no sleep I sought,
But to the field a bag of hempseed brought.
I scattered round the seed on every side,
And three times three in trembling accents cried:
"This hempseed with my virgin hand I sow;
Who shall my true love be, the crop shall mow."

I pared a pippin round and round again,
My shepherd's name to flourish in the plain;
I flung the unbroken paring o'er my head;
Upon the grass a perfect L was made.

Two hazelnuts I threw into the flame,
And to each nut I gave a sweetheart's name;
This with the loudest bounce me sore amazed,
That in a flame of brightest color blazed.
So may thy passion grow,
For 'twas thy nut that did so brightly glow.

John Gay

HALLOWE'EN

The autumn wind—oh, hear it howl!
Without—October's tempests scowl,
As he troops away on the raving wind,
And leaveth dry leaves in his path behind,
        Without—without,
        Oh, hear him shout,
    He is making the old trees bare;
        Oh, cruel he,
        To the old oak tree
    And the garden hedges fair!
Oh, a wild and tyrannous king is he
When he playeth his frolic in every tree
    And maketh the forest bare.

I know that a tyrannous rod is his
    When he maketh the forest bow;
But worse, far worse are his tyrannies,
    For he tameth the spirit now!

        Without—without,
        Oh, hear him shout,
    October is going away!
        'Tis the night—the night
        Of the grave's delight,
    And the warlocks are at their play;
        Ye think that without
        The wild winds shout,
But no, it is they—it is they.

The Spirits are pulling the sere dry leaves
    Of the shadowy forest down;
And howl the gaunt reapers that gather the sheaves,
    With the moon o'er their revels to frown.
To-morrow ye'll find all their spoils in your path,
    And ye'll speak of the wind and the sky;
But oh, could ye see them to-night in their wrath,
    I ween ye'd be frenzied of eye!

Arthur Cleveland Coxe

THE FAIRY FOLK

Come cuddle close in daddy's coat
  Beside the fire so bright,
And hear about the fairy folk
  That wander in the night.
For when the stars are shining clear
  And all the world is still,
They float across the silver moon
  From hill to cloudy hill.

Their caps of red, their cloaks of green,
  Are hung with silver bells,
And when they're shaken with the wind
  Their merry ringing swells.
And riding on the crimson moth,
  With black spots on her wings,
They guide them down the purple sky
  With golden bridle rings.

They love to visit girls and boys
  To see how sweet they sleep,
To stand beside their cosy cots
And at their faces peep.

For in the whole of fairy land
  They have no finer sight
Than little children sleeping sound
  With faces rosy bright.

On tip-toe crowding round their heads,
  When bright the moonlight beams,
They whisper little tender words
  That fill their minds with dreams;
And when they see a sunny smile,
  With lightest finger tips
They lay a hundred kisses sweet
  Upon the ruddy lips.

And then the little spotted moths
  Spread out their crimson wings,
And bear away the fairy crowd
  With shaking bridle rings.
Come, bairnies, hide in daddy's coat,
  Beside the fire so bright—
Perhaps the little fairy folk
  Will visit you to-night.

Robert Bird

Veterans Day

At the eleventh hour of the eleventh day of the eleventh month of 1918, an armistice was proclaimed that ended the hostilities of the First World War. A world almost hysterical with relief and joy celebrated spontaneously, a celebration aptly described by George William Douglas in his *American Book of Days:* "The announcement that the war was ended was flashed to all parts of the world, followed almost instantly by enthusiastic demonstrations in the cities of the United States, to say nothing of the communities in other countries which had been engaged in the conflict. Women wept and men became almost hysterical; there were impromptu parades in the streets; church bells were rung; people in offices threw ticker tape out the windows and tore telephone books into scraps and threw them on the marchers. The spontaneous rejoicing was more enthusiastic and more general than ever before known over any previous event in the history of the country. It was even greater than that of the previous week when a premature report had come from France that the armstice had been signed. That report lacked verification, but there was a feeling that the war was at an end."

Given the belief of the time that the armistice of November 11 had brought an end to the horrible slaughter of warfare *for all time,* it is easy to understand how the idea of commemorating the day annually came about. On the first anniversary of the armistice, November 11, 1919, President Woodrow Wilson issued the following proclamation:

> To my fellow-countrymen: A year ago our enemies laid down their arms in accordance with an armistice which rendered them impotent to renew hostilities, and gave to the world an assured opportunity to reconstruct its shattered order and to work out in peace a new and juster set of international relations. The soldiers and people of the European Allies had fought and endured for more than four years to uphold the barrier of civilization against the aggressions of armed force. We ourselves had been in the conflict something more than a year and a half. With splendid forgetfulness of mere personal concerns we remodeled our industries, concentrated our financial resources, increased our agricultural output, and assembled a great army, so that at the last our power was a decisive factor in the victory.

> We were able to bring the vast resources, material and moral, of a great and free people to the assistance of our associates in Europe who had suffered and sacrificed without limit in the cause for which they fought. Out of this victory there arose new possibilities of political freedom and economic concert. The war showed us the strength of great nations acting together for high purposes, and the victory of arms foretells the enduring conquests which can be made in peace when nations act justly and in furtherance of the common interests of men.

> To us in America the reflections of Armistice Day will be filled with solemn pride in the heroism of those who died in the country's service and with gratitude for the victory, both because of the thing from which it has freed us and because of the opportunity it has given America to show her sympathy with peace and justice in the councils of the nations.

For about twenty years Armistice Day was celebrated with parades of veterans and by public and religious ceremonies. Traditionally, all business was suspended for two minutes of silent meditation beginning at the eleventh hour when firing ceased at the front. But, by 1938, when President Franklin D. Roosevelt signed a law making November 11th a legal holiday in the District of Columbia, war already seemed inevitable in Europe and in Asia, making a mockery of the naive hopes of Woodrow Wilson and his "war to end all wars."

With America mourning the dead of World War II and of the Korean War, the idea of commemorating the end of the First World War seemed less and less vital as the years passed. Consequently, as Robert J. Meyers reports in *Celebrations,* "a movement began to incorporate the dead of all American wars into the observance. This was first done in Emporia Kansas, on November 11, 1953, where the day was referred to as Veterans Day. By then another 54,246 men had been entered in the lists of American war dead through the recently ended havoc of the Korean War. Representative Edward J. Rees of Emporia presented a bill in Congress in February 1954 that called for Armistice Day to be officially known henceforth as Veterans Day. The bill met no opposition and was signed into law by President Dwight D. Eisenhower on June 1, 1954."

Arlington National Cemetery (see Memorial Day) plays a significant role in the observance of Veterans Day, for it is at the Tomb of the Unknown Soldiers that the nation symbolically honors not only those fallen in combat, but those who have fought and survived. The story of the first American Unknown Soldier is well told by Gunther E. Rothenberg in *Holidays:* "To show its gratitude, and as a symbolic honor for all of the nation's dead in World War I, it was decided to bring the body of an unidentified American soldier home from the battlefields and to rebury him in Arlington National Cemetery. From American war cemeteries in France, four unidentified bodies were brought to the City Hall of Chalons-sur-Marne where Sergeant Edward S. Younger, the most decorated enlisted man of World War I, made the final choice. After praying for divine guidance, he placed a spray of white roses on one of the unmarked caskets." On November 11, 1921, at exactly 11:00 A.M., with President Warren G. Harding presiding, the Unknown Soldier was laid to rest in the Tomb below a marble marker which bears the inscription:

HERE RESTS IN HONORED GLORY
AN AMERICAN SOLDIER
KNOWN BUT TO GOD.

On Memorial Day, 1958, four years after Armistice Day became Veterans Day, the bodies of two more Unknown Soldiers were laid to rest in the Tomb. One of the Unknowns represented the dead of World War II; the other represented the dead of the Korean conflict. With the nearby graves of the assassinated Kennedy brothers suggesting the turmoil of the 1960s, one anticipates as well the imminent entombment of an Unknown from the Vietnam War.

EPICEDIUM

(IN MEMORY OF AMERICA'S DEAD IN THE GREAT WAR)

No more for them shall Evening's rose unclose,
   Nor Dawn's emblazoned panoplies be spread;
Alike, the Rain's warm kiss and stabbing snows,
   Unminded, fall upon each hallowed head.
But the Bugles, as they leap and wildly sing,
Rejoice, . . . remembering.

The gun's mad music their young ears have known—
   War's lullabies that moaned on Flanders Plain;
To-night the Wind walks on them, still as stone,
   Where they lie huddled close as riven grain.
But the Drums, reverberating, proudly roll—
They love a Soldier's soul!

With arms outflung, and eyes that laughed at Death,
   They drank the wine of sacrifice and loss;
For them a life-time spanned a burning breath,
   And Truth they visioned, clean of earthly dross.
But the Fifes,—can ye not hear their lusty shriek?
They know, and now they speak!

The lazy drift of cloud, the noon-day hum
   Of vagrant bees; the lark's untrammeled song
Shall gladden them no more, who now lie dumb
   In Death's strange sleep, yet once were swift and strong.
But the Bells, that to all living listeners peal,
With joy their deeds reveal!

They have given their lives, with bodies bruised and broken,
   Upon their Country's altar they have bled;
They have left, as priceless heritage, a token
   That Honor lives forever with the Dead.
And the Bugles, as their rich notes rise and fall—
They answer, knowing all.

J. Corson Miller

The GREATEST CRIME of THE WAR
The Torpedoing of the LUSITANIA

THE LAND

Be not afraid, O dead, be not afraid:
We have not lost the dreams that once were flung
Like pennons to the world: we yet are stung
With all the starry prophecies that made
You, on the gray dawn watchful, half afraid
Of vision. Never a night that all men sleep unstirred:
Never a sunset but the west is blurred
With banners marching, and a sign displayed.
Be not afraid, O Dead, lest we forget
A single hour your living glorified;
Come but a drum-beat, and the sleepers fret
To walk again the places where you died:
Broad is the land, our loves are broadly spread,
But now, even more widely scattered lie our dead.

O Lord of splendid nations let us dream
Not of a place of barter, nor "the State,"
But dream as lovers dream—for it is late—
Of some small place beloved; perhaps a stream
Running beside a house set round with flowers;
Perhaps a garden wet with hurrying showers,
Where bees are thick about a leaf-hid gate.
For such as these, men die nor hesitate.
The old gray cities, gossipy and wise,
The candid valleys, like a woman's brow,
The mountains treading mightily toward the skies,
Turn dreams to visions—there's a vision now!
Of hills panoplied, fields of waving spears,
And a great campus shaken with flags and tears.

Struthers Burt

IN FLANDERS FIELDS

In Flanders fields the poppies blow
Between the crosses, row on row,
   That mark our place; and in the sky
   The larks, still bravely singing, fly
Scarce heard amid the guns below.

We are the Dead. Short days ago
We lived, felt dawn, saw sunset glow,
   Loved and were loved, and now we lie
     In Flanders fields.

Take up our quarrel with the foe;
To you from falling hands we throw
   The torch; be yours to hold it high.
   If ye break faith with us who die
We shall not sleep, though poppies grow
     In Flanders fields.

John McCrae

THE UNRETURNING

For us, the dead, though young,
   For us, who fought and bled,
Let a last song be sung,
   And a last word be said!

Dreams, hopes, and high desires,
   That leaven and uplift,
On sacrificial fires
   We offered as a gift.

We gave, and gave our all,
   In gladness, though in pain;
Let not a whisper fall
   That we have died in vain!

Clinton Scollard

I HAVE A RENDEZVOUS WITH DEATH

I have a rendezvous with Death
At some disputed barricade,
When Spring comes back with rustling shade
And apple-blossoms fill the air—
I have a rendezvous with Death
When Spring brings back blue days and fair.

It may be he shall take my hand
And lead me into his dark land
And close my eyes and quench my breath—
It may be I shall pass him still.
I have a rendezvous with Death
On some scarred slope of battered hill,
When Spring comes round again this year
And the first meadow-flowers appear.

God knows 'twere better to be deep
Pillowed in silk and scented down,
Where Love throbs out in blissful sleep,
Pulse nigh to pulse, and breath to breath,
Where hushed awakenings are dear . . .
But I've a rendezvous with Death
At midnight in some flaming town,
When Spring trips north again this year,
And I to my pledged word am true,
I shall not fail that rendezvous.

Alan Seeger

THE UNKNOWN SOLDIER

They are bearing him home through the old Virginia valley,
    Home to a hill where a Nation's heroes sleep;
Hushed are the hosts that honor his silent passing.
    Hushed is their grief and deep.

Lower him tenderly; vex not his gentle dreaming;
    Pillow his head on the kindly loam of France.
So shall his sleep be the sweeter, feeling thy nearness,
    Land of the Great Romance.

Souls of the mighty fallen stand at attention,
    Sheridan riding his shadowy steed of fame;
Heroes of Gettysburg, Shiloh, and grim Shenandoah,
    Scorched in the battle flame;
A hundred score of lads whose bodies were taken
    Maimed from the fields where the red Rappahannock runs;
Nameless as he, yet honored as he is honored;
    All of them Mothers' Sons!

He is the youth of America, taken untimely;
    Symbol of countless thousands who perished young;
Sinew and bone of a Nation, crushed in the making;
    The poet, his song half sung.
You, who dwell in a liberty bought by his passing,
    It is your Son, your Brother is buried here.
Pause for a moment, forgetting the day's occupation,
    Offer a prayer—a tear.

Vilda Sauvage Owens

Thanksgiving

Although a day reserved for general thanksgiving—especially at harvest time—has been observed by almost every nation in almost every period, Thanksgiving Day as observed in the United States has evolved as a unique American feast.

Probably the first thanksgiving service in America was that held on May 27, 1578, by the members of the expedition under Frobisher, on the shores of Newfoundland. This was conducted by an English minister named Wolfall, who preached a thanksgiving sermon. The first record of a thanksgiving service within the limits of the present United States, however, was that held by the members of the Popham colony who settled on the coast of Maine in August, 1607. According to some authorities, a thanksgiving service was held by the Pilgrims as early as December, 1620, soon after the landing of the Mayflower.

Those, however, were merely thanksgiving services, and the origin of a *day* of thanksgiving such as we now celebrate must be attributed to Governor Bradford of Plymouth. In November, 1620, the Pilgrims landed on the desolate coast of New England and passed the following winter with great suffering and privation. In the spring, seed was sown and its growth was watched with great anxiety, for on the result depended the lives of the colonists. When the grain was cut and the harvest was found to be abundant, there was great rejoicing, and the governor proclaimed a day of thanksgiving. He sent out four men in search of game, and they soon returned with a large number of wild fowl, most of which were turkeys. It is doubtless due to this incident that the turkey has always been considered a necessary feature of Thanksgiving Day feasts. (Robert J. Meyers repeats the doubtful, but amusing, story of how the turkey "is said to have gotten its name from the doctor on Columbus' first voyage, Luis de Torres, who exclaimed *"Tukki!"* on seeing the unusual fowl for the first time. This is Hebrew for 'big bird.' " (One imagines that *Sesame Street*'s famous Big Bird would resent being called a turkey!)

The Plymouth Thanksgiving festival lasted nearly a week and a large party of friendly Indians, including the chief Massasoit, shared in the festivities. The bill of fare for this first Thanksgiving feast has not been handed down to us, but it doubtless consisted of turkeys, ducks, and geese. The Indians furnished venison and probably other game. The vegetables appear to have been the same as those now used at Thanksgiving: native squash and pumpkin. The provisions must have been abundant, for about 140 persons, including 90 Indians, were entertained for three days. The exact date of this festival is not known, but according to the records it must have occurred between September 23rd and November 11th, probably in October, 1621.

In the summer of 1623 the little colony was again facing starvation. A drought which had begun in May and continued for six long weeks had almost destroyed the crops. About the middle of July, the governor appointed a day for fasting and prayer. Soon after this the weather changed and a gentle rain set in which lasted for several days, saving the crops and reviving the spirits of the settlers. About the same time, Captain Miles Standish returned from a voyage which he had taken to secure provisions and brought with him not only much needed food, but also news that a ship which was expected from Holland had been sighted and would soon arrive. In acknowledgement of these blessings, a day of thanksgiving and prayer was appointed and held on July 30, 1623. Some writers claim that the festival held in 1623 was the origin of our Thanksgiving Day, because it was a religious as well as a social celebration, while the feast held in 1621 was rather an occasion of festivity and merrymaking, there being no special religious observance on that occasion. It is probable, however, that both these celebrations had their influence in forming our present Thanksgiving Day.

In September, 1789, Elias Boudinot moved in the House of Representatives that President Washington be requested to recommend "a day of thanksgiving and prayer to be observed by the people of the United States in acknowledgment of the favors of the Almighty God, and especially His affording them the opportunity peaceably to establish a constitution of government for their safety and happiness." There was some objection, but the motion was carried, and on October 3, 1789, Washington issued a proclamation appointing Thursday, November 26, 1789, as a day of general thanksgiving. This was the first thanksgiving proclamation issued by a United States president, and this day may be considered the first national Thanksgiving Day.

Thanksgiving days were irregularly celebrated in the following three-quarters of a century, and almost never in the South. But in 1864, President Lincoln issued a proclamation appointing the fourth Thursday in November, with a view of having the day observed every year thereafter. The very next year, however, the assassination of Lincoln almost caused a suspension of this rule, but President Andrew Johnson was prevailed upon to follow Lincoln's wishes, and since then each president (with one exception) has followed this custom. In 1939 and 1940, Franklin D. Roosevelt, yielding to the pressures of businessmen who wanted a longer Christmas selling season, appointed the *third* Thursday in November as Thanksgiving Day. This so upset the sensibilities of custom-conscious Americans that, through a Congressional Joint Resolution, the observance was returned to the fourth Thursday in 1941.

The adoption of the last Thursday in November as a uniform date for the observance of Thanksgiving was largely due to the efforts of Mrs. Sarah J. Hale, a prominent American author of the nineteenth century and editor of the popular magazine *Godey's Lady's Book*. About 1840 she began agitating for a more general observance of the day and the selection of a definite time, so that the celebration might have a more national character. Year after year she wrote to the governors of the states asking them to appoint the last Thursday in November. The idea met with general approval and this finally led to the adoption of the present method of fixing the date.

Thanksgiving Day is observed by feasting and general festivity, and remains one of the greatest home festivals of the year and a day of family reunions. The electronic era of television has, however, resulted in millions of Americans being thankful for the broadcast of football games rather than for the bounties of nature that brought about Thanksgiving Day in the first place.

THE TURKEYS' HOLIDAYS.

AN ACROSTIC

T   *is for Turkeys, so great and renowned;*
H   *for the Hearth, that we gather around.*
A   *for the Apples, so rosy and sweet;*
N   *for the Nuts that are always a treat;*
K   *for the Kindling we burn in the grate;*
S   *for the Stories our elders relate.*
G   *for the Games, when the feasting is o'er;*
I   *for the Icicles outside the door;*
V   *for the Vigilant Fathers of old,*
I   *for Ideals, they taught us to hold.*
N   *for the Needy we meet here and there;*
G   *for the Gifts and the "Goodies" we share.*

Mabel Livingston Frank

THE KING OF FESTIVALS

The king and high priest of all festivals was the autumn Thanksgiving. When the apples were all gathered and the cider was all made and the yellow pumpkins were rolled in from many a hill in billows of gold, and the corn was husked, and the labors of the season were done, and the warm, late days of Indian Summer came in, dreamy, and calm, and still, with just enough frost to crisp the ground of a morning, but with warm traces of benignant, sunny hours at noon, there came over the community a sort of genial repose of spirit—a sense of something accomplished, and of a new golden mark made in advance,—and the deacon began to say to the minister, of a Sunday, "I suppose it's about time for the Thanksgiving proclamation."

Harriet Beecher Stowe.

THE FIRST
THANKSGIVING DAY

In Puritan New England a year had passed away
Since first beside the Plymouth coast the English Mayflower lay,
When Bradford, the good Governor, sent fowlers forth to snare
The turkey and the wild-fowl, to increase the scanty fare:—

"Our husbandry hath prospered, there is corn enough for food,
Though 'the pease be parched in blossom, and the grain indifferent good.'
Who blessed the loaves and fishes for the feast miraculous,
And filled with oil the widow's cruse, He hath remembered us!

"Give thanks unto the Lord of Hosts, by whom we all are fed,
Who granted us our daily prayer, 'Give us our daily bread!'
By us and by our children let this day be kept for aye,
In memory of His bounty, as the land's Thanksgiving Day."

Each brought his share of Indian meal the pious feast to make,
With the fat deer from the forest and the wild-fowl from the brake.
And chanted hymn and prayer were raised—though eyes with tears were dim—
"The Lord He hath remembered us, let us remember Him!"

Then Bradford stood up at their head and lifted up his voice:
"The corn is gathered from the field, I call you to rejoice;
Thank God for all His mercies, from the greatest to the least,
Together have we *fasted*, friends, together let us *feast*.

"The Lord who led forth Israel was with us in the waste;
Sometime in light, sometime in cloud, before us He hath paced;
Now give Him thanks, and pray to Him who holds us in His hand
To prosper us and make of this a strong and mighty land!". . .

From Plymouth to the Golden Gate to-day their children tread,
The mercies of that bounteous Hand upon the land are shed;
The "flocks are on a thousand hills," the prairies wave with grain,
The cities spring like mushrooms now where once was desert-plain.

Heap high the board with plenteous cheer and gather to the feast,
And toast that sturdy Pilgrim band whose courage never ceased.
Give praise to that All-Gracious One by whom their steps were led,
And thanks unto the harvest's Lord who sends our "daily bread."

Alice Williams Brotherton

THANKSGIVING MEMORIES

Thanksgiving! What a world of pleasant memories the word recalls; memories obscured and softened not by the mists of time but by the odorous steam rising slowly from innumerable savory dishes! Oh, the Thanksgiving dinners we have eaten; the Thanksgiving cheer of which we have partaken! We smile when we think of them, and our eyes grow misty and our hearts tender; for, alas, many who in days that are gone sat down with us at table will do so never again, and many a hand that was outstretched to us in greeting is stilled forever.

But this tinge of sorrow serves only to make our memories of those days more sweet and tender. November has come. There is a chill in the air, and in the early morning the meadows are white with frost. Then, one afternoon, a bank of dark gray clouds appears in the north, and rolls down across the sky, and presently the white flakes are falling fast. By evening, the old brown, toil-scarred earth has been clothed in a mantle of spotless white; and when morning dawns, the snow is heaped high over hill and dale. The world is ready for Thanksgiving.

And we are ready, too. For days and days, preparations have been afoot indoors. The house has been pervaded with sweet and tantalizing odors; and when, at last, the evening before the great day, we steal to the cupboard doors and slyly peep within, what a sight greets the enchanted eye! There, on the topmost shelf, are the pumpkin pies, six of them, fat and juicy, odorous with their spicy contents, baked to a turn. Then there are the preserves and jellies set out ready for the feast—in especial, a certain marmalade, made of currants and red raspberries and I know not what besides, of a flavor to ravish and delight the most indifferent palate.

And there, on the lower shelf, is the turkey,—a few short hours before the ruffled and vainglorious King of the Barnyard, with no slightest suspicion of the fate in store for him; now plucked clean, and stuffed with spiced bread and oysters, his wings turned in and his legs trussed together, waiting to occupy the place of honor at the morrow's banquet.

The great day dawns clear and fair and pleasantly cold. Long before sunrise the house has been astir, for the preparation of the feast is no light affair, to be accomplished in a few hours. The kitchen range is aglow, and into the capacious oven goes the great turkey. To one of the children is assigned the task of "basting" him—of opening the oven door, from time to time, and dipping over his browning bosom some gravy from the pan in which he rests—and every time the oven door is opened the others in the kitchen must cluster around to get a glimpse of him and to sniff the ravishing aroma.

Meanwhile the guests have been arriving—cousins, uncles, aunts, nephews, nieces,—and such a bevy of bright-eyed, red-cheeked children as makes the old house ring from end to end. A sentry has to be stationed at the kitchen door to keep them out. The women take off their wraps and hasten to the kitchen to offer assistance; the men sit around the fire in the parlor and discuss the season, the crops, and the news of the neighborhood. The clock on the mantle ticks noisily on, and just as its hands come together at the stroke of twelve, the door into the dining-room is thrown open, and the women smilingly announce that dinner is ready.

Oh, what a spectacle that board affords, with its snowy cloth, its shining porcelain, its gleaming silver! And oh, what delights await the palate! "Now may digestion wait on appetite and health on both!" But grandfather, who has taken his accustomed place at the table-head, pauses a moment and glances around with tender eyes at the happy faces before him. A silence falls, and heads are bent as, in a low and reverent voice, he says, "Let us pray."

John Tremaine.

THANKSGIVING

What can be sweeter than the wholesome fragrance of the fallen leaves? What more invigorating than the breath of the two seasons that we catch: here in the northward shade of a wooded hill the nipping air of winter, there where the southern slope meets the sun the genial warmth of an October day? Here one's footsteps crunch sharply the frozen herbage and ice-bearded border of a spring's overflow; there splash in thawed pools and rustle softly among the dead leaves.

The flowers are gone, but they were not brighter than the winter berries and bittersweet that glow around one. The deciduous leaves are fallen and withered, but they were not more beautiful than the delicate tracery of their forsaken branches, and the steadfast foliage of the evergreens was never brighter. The song-birds are singing in southern woods, but chickadee, nuthatch, and woodpecker are chatty and companionable and keep the woods in heart with a stir of life.

Far off one hears the intermittent discharge of rifles where the shooters are burning powder for their Thanksgiving turkey, and faintly from far away comes the melancholy music of a hound. Then the hound goes by, and footsteps, voice, and echo sink into silence. For silence it is, though the silver tinkle of the brook is in it, and the stir of the last leaf shivering forsaken on its bough.

In such quietude one may hold heartfelt thanksgiving, feasting full upon a crust and a draft from the icy rivulet, and leave rich viands and costly wines for the thankless surfeiting of poorer men.

Rowland E. Robinson.

BILLY AND
MISTER TURKEY

'Twas on a dull November day,
When Billy, on his homeward way,
Met Mister Turkey, whom he knew,
And stopped to have a word or two.

Said Billy: "Thursday's drawing nigh,
With turkey (roast) and pumpkin-pie,
And many kinds of first-class fare—
But don't you worry—*you'll* be there!"

Now whether Mister Turkey knew
What Billy meant, I leave to you;
But he said, *"Gobble!"* trailed his wing,
And Billy ran like anything!

Katherine M. Daland

A THANKSGIVING CELEBRATION IN 1779

When Thanksgiving Day was approaching, our dear Grandmother Smith, who is sometimes a little desponding of spirit as you well know, did her best to persuade us that it would be better to make it a day of fasting and prayer in view of the *wickedness of our friends and the vileness of our enemies;* but my dear father brought her to a more proper frame of mind, so that by the time the day came she was ready to enjoy it almost as well as Grandmother Worthington did, and she, you will remember, always sees the bright side.

This year it was Uncle Simeon's turn to have the dinner at his house. The tables were set in the dining hall and even that big room had no space to spare when we were all seated. Of course we could have no roast beef. None of us have tasted beef this three years back, as it must all go to the army, and too little they get, poor fellows. But we had a good haunch of venison on each table. These were balanced by huge chines of roast pork at the other ends of the tables. Then there was on one a big roast turkey and on the other a goose and two big pigeon pasties, and an abundance of vegetables of all the old sorts, and one which I do not believe you have yet seen. It is called celery and you eat it without cooking. It is very good served with meats.

Our mince pies were good and the pumpkin pies, apple tarts and big Indian pudding, lacked for nothing save *appetite* by the time we got round to them. Of course we had no wine. Uncle Simeon still has a cask or two, but it must all be saved for the sick, and indeed, for those who are well, good cider is a sufficient substitute.

The day was bitter cold, and when we got home from meeting we were glad enough of the big fire in uncle's dining hall, but by the time the dinner was one half over those of us who were on the fire side of one table were forced to get up and carry our plates with us around to the far side of the other table, while those who had sat there, were as glad to bring their plates around to the fire side to get warm.

Uncle Simeon was in his best mood, and you know how good that is! He kept both tables in a roar of laughter with his droll stories of the days when he was studying medicine in Edinboro.

Then we all sang a hymn, and afterwards my dear father led us in prayer, remembering all absent friends before the Throne of Grace.

We did not rise from the table until it was quite dark, and then when the dishes had been cleared away, we all got round the fire as close as we could, and cracked nuts, and sang songs, and told stories. You know nobody could exceed the two Grandmothers at telling tales of all the things they have seen themselves, and repeating those of the early years in New England, and even some in Old England, which they had heard in their youth from their elders. My father says it is a goodly custom to hand down all worthy deeds and traditions from father to son, because the word that is spoken is remembered longer than the one that is written.

Juliana Smith.

From a letter written in 1779.

THE PUMPKIN

Ah! on Thanksgiving Day, when from East and from West,
From North and from South come the pilgrim and guest,
When the gray-haired New Englander sees round his board,
The old broken links of affection restored,
When the care-wearied man seeks his mother once more,
And the worn matron smiles where the girl smiled before,
What moistens the lip and what brightens the eye?
What calls back the past, like the rich Pumpkin pie?

Oh, fruit loved of boyhood! the old days recalling,
When wood-grapes were purpling and brown nuts were falling!
When wild, ugly faces we carved in its skin,
Glaring out through the dark with a candle within!
When we laughed round the corn-heap, with hearts all in tune,
Our chair a broad pumpkin,—our lantern the moon,
Telling tales of the fairy who travelled like steam,
In a pumpkin-shell coach, with two rats for her team!

Then thanks for thy present! none sweeter or better
E'er smoked from an oven or circled a platter!
Fairer hands never wrought at a pastry more fine,
Brighter eyes never watched o'er its baking, than thine!
And the prayer, which my mouth is too full to express,
Swells my heart that thy shadow may never be less,
That the days of thy lot may be lengthened below,
And the fame of thy worth like a pumpkin-vine grow,
And thy life be as sweet, and its last sunset sky
Golden-tinted and fair as thy own Pumpkin pie!

John Greenleaf Whittier

HOME TO THANKSGIVING.

THANKSGIVING DAY

Over the river and through the wood,
  To grandfather's house we'll go;
    The horse knows the way
    To carry the sleigh
  Through the white and drifted snow.

Over the river and through the wood,—
  Oh, how the wind does blow!
    It stings the toes
    And bites the nose
  As over the ground we go.

Over the river and through the wood,
  To have a first-rate play,
    Hear the bells ring,
    "Ting-a-ling-ding!"
  Hurrah for Thanksgiving Day!

Over the river and through the wood
  Trot fast, my dapple gray!
    Spring over the ground
    Like a hunting hound!
  For this is Thanksgiving Day.

Over the river and through the wood,
  And straight throigh the barn-yard gate;
    We seem to go
    Extremely slow;
  It is so hard to wait!

Over the river and through the wood,
  Now grandmother's cap I spy!
    Hurrah for the fun!
    Is the pudding done?
  Hurrah for the pumpkin pie!

Lydia Maria Child

GIVING THANKS

For the hay and the corn and wheat that is reaped,
For the labor well done, and the barns that are heaped,
For the sun and the dew and the sweet honey-comb,
For the rose and the song, and the harvest brought home—
     Thanksgiving!   Thanksgiving!

For the trade and the skill and the wealth in our land,
For the cunning and strength of the workingman's hand,
For the good that our artists and poets have taught,
For the friendship that hope and affection have brought—
     Thanksgiving!   Thanksgiving!

For the homes that with purest affection are blest,
For the season of plenty and well deserved rest,
For our country extending from sea to sea,
The land that is known as the "Land of the Free"—
     Thanksgiving!   Thanksgiving!

Anonymous

Christmas

Christmas is the most important holiday in the American year. Although it is a Christian festival day—the very term "Christmas" simply meaning "Christ's mass"—it has become over the years as secular a festival as any other. It is perhaps inevitable that this should have happened. Christmas falls at the darkest time of the year; on the 22nd of December the sun reaches its lowest point in the Northern hemisphere. From this time on it slowly begins its ascent toward the Spring solstice of March. Ancient peoples, more closely attuned to the almost imperceptible changes of the seasons, celebrated the return of heavenly light in the month of December. The Hebrews, too, recognized the movement of the sun in relation to the earth in their Festival of Lights or Hannukah. With the spread of Christianity throughout the Western world, this most natural of celebrations assumed a different form. The birth of Jesus was ascribed to December 25th. Whether this date is, indeed, the correct one will always remain an historical mystery, but it is surely an appropriate time for the coming of the Messiah. The star of Bethlehem shone upon the earth with a special brilliance, a symbol of the retreat of winter darkness and a beacon to light the way to a rebirth of the spirit.

In the United States Christmas customs from all regions of the Western world came together in a unique blend. The first celebrations were stoutly resisted by the dissenting Protestants of New England, just as they were by early Christians who found something pagan and unspiritual in the merrymaking of the season. As late as 1874, Congregationalist Henry Ward Beecher explained that the holiday was one that was alien to his New England soul:

> To me Christmas is a foreign day, and I shall die so. When I was a boy I wondered what Christmas was. I knew there was such a time, because we had an Episcopal church in our town, and I saw them dressing it with evergreens, and wondered what they were taking the woods in church for; but I got no satisfactory explanation. A little later I understood it was a Romish institution, kept up by the Romish Church. Brought up in the strictest State of New England, brought up in the most literal style of worship, brought up where they would not read the Bible in church because the Episcopalians read it so much, I passed all my youth without any knowledge of Christmas, and so I have no associations with the day. Where the Christmas revel ought to be, I have nothing. It is Christmas Day, that is all.

One can only pity this loss. It was, of course, not experienced at the time by many American young people. During the years of Beecher's childhood--from 1813 to, roughly, the 1830s—Christmas was being celebrated quite festively in nearly all areas of North America. The singing of carols, decorating homes and churches with evergreen boughs, mistletoe, and holly, and the giving of small gifts were British customs natural to many families, especially those of the Anglican persuasion. The Dutch of New Amsterdam—as Calvinistic in many ways as the New Englanders—were, nevertheless, stout defenders of the kindly figure of St. Nicholas, or Santa Claus (a diminutive form of Sinterklass or Sint Nikolaas) who visited children with gifts on December 6th. By the early years of the nineteenth century, the

German settlers in Pennsylvania introduced the Christmas tree and their own traditional story of the Christ child—Christkindl—who bears gifts to good children on Christmas Eve.

By the mid-1800s these varied traditions were beginning to blend together in the form we know today. St. Nicholas's festival day was still observed in Holland on the 6th, but in North America the visitation of Santa Claus was moved to the evening of the 24th. And, to the horror of many devout Christians, Christkindl was corrupted to the form of Kriss Kringle. As one historian of holidays has noted, "There was no going back and there was no untangling; Kriss Kringle was Santa Claus was St. Nicholas and still is."

The Christmas tree became even more popular a symbol in America after it had been introduced in England by Prince Albert in the 1840s. Popular magazines of the period began to feature pictures of beautifully decorated trees. Perhaps most important, writers such as Charles Dickens devoted considerable time to the creation of tales of the Christmas spirit. These stories have since become as much a part of tradition as boughs of holly and the giving of gifts. So, too, were carols introduced at the time. Songs of the Christmas season always existed, but by the mid-nineteenth century, such new classics as "Silent Night," "O, Little Town of Bethlehem," and "Hark, the Herald Angels Sing" were being enjoyed by people of all Christian faiths.

It was thus inevitable that the festival of Christmas should not only survive prohibition but actually assume a new and vigorous form in America. And it was probably certain that the holiday should become so very commercialized over the years. Only in the United States did Santa Claus emerge as such a very beneficent figure. The British held on to their simple "Father Christmas"; the French their "Père Noël." But here Santa was to pop up on almost every street corner during the month of December, leading no small number of children to wonder about his extraordinary mobility. The sending of Christmas cards began in England in the mid-1800s and quickly became a giant business in America. Today there is a beginning of a retreat from some of the gaudier and commercially crass forms of celebration. It is unlikely, however, that Christ shall ever return to Christmas in the way celebrated in simpler days. The early Christians and the later Puritans were not entirely amiss in their opposition to festive Christmas rites. They understood that people everywhere will use any excuse they can invent to break the monotony of daily existence and that others will seize upon this need to profit from the general merriment. But just as there is no way to darken the growing light announced by the winter solstice, there is no possible manner of rolling back customs which have grown over a period of time. And despite the emphasis on material rewards which accompanies so much of American Christmas practice, something of the simple charity and hope symbolized at Bethlehem remains to gladden the hearts of all people at this one time of the year.

MERRY CHRISTMAS

M for the	Music, merry and clear;
E for the	Eve, the crown of the year-
R for the	Romping of bright girls and boys;
R for the	Reindeer that bring them the toys;
Y for the	Yule-log softly aglow.
C for the	Cold of the sky and the snow;
H for the	Hearth where they hang up the hose;
R for the	Reel which the old folks propose;
I for the	Icicles seen through the pane;
S for the	Sleigh-bells, with tinkling refrain;
T for the	Tree with gifts all a-bloom
M for the	Mistletoe hung in the room;
A for the	Anthems we all love to hear;
S for	St. Nicholas—joy of the year!

St. Nicholas (January, 1897)

CHRISTMAS THOUGHTS

Of all the old festivals, that of Christmas awakens the strongest and most heartfelt associations. There is a tone of solemn and sacred feeling that blends with our conviviality and lifts the spirit to a state of hallowed and elevated enjoyment.

It is a beautiful arrangement, derived from days of yore, that this festival, which commemorates the announcement of the religion of peace and love, has been made the season for gathering together of family connections, and drawing closer again those bands of kindred hearts which the cares, and pleasures, and sorrows of the world are continually operating to cast loose; of calling back the children of a family, who have launched forth in life, once more to assemble about the paternal hearth, there to grow young and loving again among the endearing mementos of childhood.

There is something in the very season of the year that gives a charm to the festivity of Christmas. In the depth of winter, when Nature lies despoiled of her charms, wrapt in her shroud of sheeted snow, we turn for our gratifications to moral sources. Heart calleth unto heart, and we draw our pleasures from the deep wells of living kindness which lie in the quiet recesses of our bosoms.

Amidst the general call to happiness, the bustle of the spirits and stir of the affections, which prevail at this period, what bosom can remain insensible? It is indeed the season of regenerated feeling—the season for kindling not merely the fire of hospitality in the hall, but the genial flame of charity in the heart. He who can turn churlishly away from contemplating the felicity of his fellow-beings and can sit down repining in loneliness, when all around is joyful, wants the genial and social sympathies which constitute the charm of a merry Christmas.

Washington Irving.
From "The Sketch-Book."

THE STARS

The stars are lighted candles
   Upon a Christmas tree
(The branches that they hang upon
   We cannot ever see)
On Christmas Eve the angels stand
   About it after tea,
And if an angel's very good
He gets a present, as he should.

Mary Carolyn Davies

THE ANGEL'S STORY

Through the blue and frosty heavens
  Christmas stars were shining bright;
Glistening lamps throughout the city
  Almost matched their gleaming light;
While the winter snow was lying,
And the winter winds were sighing,
  Long ago, one Christmas night.

While from every tower and steeple
  Pealing bells were sounding clear,
(Never were such tones of gladness
  Save when Christmas time is near),
Many a one that night was merry
  Who had toiled through all the year.

That night saw old wrongs forgiven,
  Friends, long parted, reconciled;
Voices all unused to laughter,
  Mournful eyes that rarely smiled,
Trembling hearts that feared the morrow,
  From their anxious thoughts beguiled.

Rich and poor felt love and blessing
  From the gracious season fall;
Joy and plenty in the cottage,
  Peace and feasting in the hall;
And the voices of the children
  Ringling clear above it all!

Adelaide Anne Procter

A Christmas Wish.

The bird ascending high in air
Wishes you every good may share.

A Merry Christmas to you.

A Christmas Wish

May your Christmas tree
be a heavy one.
But your heart a light one
And every gift the right
one
On this Christmas Day.

C-160

CHRISTMAS CUSTOMS
AND SUPERSTITIONS

There is always something fascinating about the folklore of holidays and festivals; and when such legends are based upon pleasant conceits, they became of double interest. Despite the whirling of time, the good old traditions linger with us, especially those which cluster about the Christmas season.

A quaint belief, peculiar to England, holds that any person turning a mattress on Christmas Day will die within a year; but it is praiseworthy to bake bread on Christmas Eve, and loaves baked then will never go moldy.

In Germany, on Christmas Eve, the whole household prepares for church, where a simple but impressive service is always held. The worshipers are always armed with lighted candles, and the first comer will find the church in darkness. He places his lighted candle before him; and as one after another appears, fresh candles flash out, till the building resembles a large parterre of single flames. The service over, the season is supposed to have fairly begun, and Christmas greetings are heard on every side.

The Christmas feeding of the birds is prevalent in many of the provinces of Norway and Sweden. Bunches of oats are placed on the roofs of houses, on trees and fences, for them to feed upon. Every poor man and every head of a family saves a penny or two to buy a bunch of oats for the birds to have their Christmas. It is a beautiful custom and one that might well be adopted in other countries.

From time immemorial, unwonted energy and sagacity have been attributed to the cock at the Christmas season. In England and in this country, one often hears the remark, "The cock is crowing for Christmas," when his clear challenge rings out in the still December nights. He is supposed to do this for the purpose of frightening away evil spirits, so that they may not disturb this holy season.

In the German Alps, it is believed that horses and cattle have the gift of language on Christmas Eve, and tell each other of the great event which the day commemorates. But it is a sin to attempt to overhear them. The story is told of a farmer's servant who did not believe that the cattle could speak, and in order to make sure, he hid in his master's stable on Christmas Eve and listened. Just as the clock struck, one horse said, "We shall have heavy work to do this day." "Yes," said the other, "the way to the church yard is long and steep." The servant was buried that day.

In Poland and elsewhere it is believed that on Christmas night the skies are opened, and Jacob's ladder is again extended from earth to heaven, but only the saints can see it.

In Austria, candles are placed in the windows, so that the Christ-Child may not stumble in passing along the road.

Scandinavia is especially the land of the Yule log of Christmas stories and legends of Thor and Odin. Then is the time for skating, sledging, dancing, and a general frolic. It is customary for every member of the family to take a bath on the afternoon preceding Christmas, and it is often the only thorough bath which is taken during the year. A pretty symbol of the spirit that reigns is the custom of placing in a row every pair of shoes in each household, to signify that during the year the family will live together in harmony and peace.

Anonymous

CHRISTMAS—GATHERING EVERGREENS.

CHRISTMAS JOY

Hark! the ringing of bells, glad Christmas bells, seems to well out the sound—"Peace on earth,
good-will to men!"

Happy voices carol the song, "Good tidings of glad joy!" And the silvery laughter of children
echoes the refrain.

Fair forms gather at the Christmas feast, while the sprays of mistletoe and holly give greeting to all.

Beneath the glow and glitter of lights, the dancers swing, with sparkling eyes and rose-hued cheeks.

And, towering over all, in its radiant beauty, splendid with gifts for everyone, stands the Christmas-tree.

Shout upon shout breaks out upon the snowy air; and the Christ-child, listening, smiles His blessing.

Rosamond Livingstone McNaught.

THE CHRISTMAS SPIRIT

What is the Christmas spirit?

It is the spirit which brings a smile to the lips and tenderness to the heart; it is the spirit which warms one into friendship with all the world, which impels one to hold out the hand of fellowship to every man and woman.

For the Christmas motto is "Peace on earth, good-will to men," and the spirit of Christmas demands that it ring in our hearts and find expression in kindly acts and loving words.

What a joyful thing for the world it would be if the Christmas spirit could do this, not only on that holiday, but on every day of the year. What a beautiful place the world would be to live in! Peace and good-will everywhere and always! Let each one of us resolve that, so far as we are concerned, peace and good-will shall be our motto every day, and that we will do our best to make the Christmas spirit last all the year round.

Anonymous

HAULING HOME THE CHRISTMAS BOUGHS.—[Drawn by H. W. Herrick.]

RECOLLECTIONS OF
MY CHRISTMAS TREE

I have been looking on, this evening, at a merry company of children assembled round that pretty
German toy, a Christmas tree.

Being now at home again, and alone, the only person in the house awake, my thoughts are drawn back,
by a fascination which I do not care to resist, to my own childhood. Straight in the middle of the room,
cramped in the freedom of its growth by no encircling walls or soon-reached ceiling, a shadowy tree
arises; and, looking up in to the dreamy brightness of its top,—for I observe in this tree the singular
property that it appears to grow downward toward the earth,—I look into my youngest Christmas
recollections.

All toys at first, I find. But upon the branches of the tree, lower down, how thick the books begin to
hang! Thin books, in themselves, at first, but many of them, with deliciously smooth covers of bright
red and green. What fat black letters to begin with!

"A was an archer, and shot at a frog." Of course he was. He was an apple-pie also, and there he is! He
was a good many things in his time, was A, and so were most of his friends, except X, who had so little
versatility that I never knew him to get beyond Xerxes or Xantippe; like Y, who was always confined to
a yacht or a yew-tree; and Z, condemned forever to be a zebra or a zany.

But now the very tree itself changes, and becomes a beanstalk,—the marvelous bean-stalk by which Jack
climbed up to the giant's house. Jack,—how noble, with his sword of sharpness and his shoes of
swiftness!

Good for Christmas-time is the ruddy color of the cloak in which, the tree making a forest of itself for
her to trip through with her basket, Little Red Ridinghood comes to me one Christmas eve to give me
information of the cruelty and treachery of that dissembling wolf who ate her grandmother, without
making any impression on his appetite and then ate her, after making that ferocious joke about his teeth.

She was my first love. I felt that if I could have married Little Red Ridinghood I should have known
perfect bliss. But it was not to be, and there was nothing for it but to look out the wolf in the Noah's
ark there, and put him last in the procession on the table, as a monster who was to be degraded.

Oh! the wonderful Noah's Ark! It was not found seaworthy when put in a washing-tub, and the animals
were crammed in at the roof and needed to have their legs well shaken down before they could be got in
even there; and then ten to one but they began to tumble out at the door, which was but imperfectly
fastened with a wire latch; but what was that against it?

Consider the noble fly, a size or two smaller than the elephant; the lady-bird, the butterfly,—all
triumphs of art! Consider the goose, whose feet were so small and whose balance was so indifferent that
he usually tumbled forward and knocked down all the animal creation! Consider Noah and his family,
like idiotic tobacco-stoppers; and how the leopard stuck to warm little fingers; and how the tails of the
larger animals used gradually to resolve themselves into frayed bits of string.

Hush! Again a forest, and somebody up in a tree,—not Robin Hood, not Valentine, not the Yellow
Dwarf,—I have passed him and all Mother Bunch's wonders without mention,—but an Eastern King
with the glittering scimetar and turban. It is the setting-in of the bright Arabian knights.

Oh, now all common things become uncommon and enchanted to me! All lamps are wonderful! All rings
are talismans! Common flower-pots are full of treasure, with a little earth scattered on the top; trees are
for Ali Baba to hide in; beefsteaks are to throw down into the Valley of Diamonds, that the precious

stones may stick to them, and be carried by the eagles to their nests, whence the traders, with loud cries, will scare them. All the dates imported come from the same tree as that unlucky one with whose shell the merchant knocked out the eye of the genii's invisible son. All olives are of the same stalk of that fresh fruit concerning which the Commander of the Faithful overheard the boy conduct the fictitious trial of the fraudulent merchant. Yes, on every object that I recognize among those upper branches of my Christmas tree I see this fairy light.

But hark! The Waits are playing, and they break my childish sleep! What images do I associate with the Christmas music, as I see them set forth on the Christmas tree! Known before all the others, keeping far apart from all the others, they gather round my little bed. An angel, speaking to a group of shepherds in a field; some travelers, with eyes uplifted, following a star; a baby in a manger; a child in a spacious temple, talking with grave men; a solemn figure with a mild and beautiful face, raising a dead girl by the hand; again, near a city gate, calling back the son of a widow, on his bier, to life; a crowd of people looking through the open roof of a chamber where He sits, and letting down a sick person on a bed, with ropes; the same, in a tempest, walking on the waters; in a ship again, on a sea-shore, teaching a great multitude; again with a child upon his knee, and other children around; again, restoring sight to the blind, speech to the dumb, hearing to the deaf, health to the sick, strength to the lame, knowledge to the ignorant; again, dying upon a cross, watched by armed soldiers, a darkness coming on, the earth beginning to shake, and only one voice heard, "Forgive them, for they know not what they do!" Encircled by the social thoughts of Christmas time, still let the benignant figure of my childhood stand unchanged! In every cheerful image and suggestion that the season brings, may the bright star that rested above the poor roof be the star of all Christian world!

A moment's pause, O vanishing tree, of which the lower boughs are dark to me yet, and let me look once more. I know there are blank spaces on thy branches, where eyes that I have loved have shone and smiled, from which they are departed. But, far above, I see the raiser of the dead girl and the widow's son—and God is good!

Charles Dickens

EARLY CHRISTMAS MORNING

Four little feet pattering on the floor,
Two tangled curly heads peeping at the door,
Hear the merry laughter, happy childish roar,
    Early Christmas morning.

Two little stockings full of sweets and toys,
Everything charming for little girls and boys.
How could they help, then, making such a noise?
    Early Christmas morning.

Down beside the stockings many gifts were spread,
Dollies, drums, a cradle and a brand new sled.
"Haven't we too many?" little Nellie said,
    Early Christmas morning.

Four little bare feet on the sidewalk cold,
Two little faces with want and hunger old
Peeping through the window where those gifts unrolled,
    Early Christmas morning.

"Yes," says John to Nellie, as he spied the two,
"We've so many presents, tell you what we'll do.
I'll give half of mine away. Now, dear Nell, will you?"
    Early Christmas morning.

Two little famished ones in the house were called,
Favors heaped upon them till they stood enthralled.
Was not this the angel's song, "Peace, good-will to all?"
    Early Christmas morning.

—*Mary B. Peck.*

WHAT DOES JOHNNY WANT?

Dear Santa Claus:
I don't want a thing that girls would like;
I don't want a velocipede, but a bike;
I don't want a gun that will not shoot;
I don't want an engine that won't toot;
I don't want mittens for the snow;
I dont't want a horse-car that won't go;
I don't want anything to wear;
I don't want an apple or a pear;
I don't want anything made of tin;
I don't want a top that will not spin;
I don't want any book I can't use;
I don't want a best pair of shoes;
I don't want a ship that won't sail;
I don't want a goody-goody tale;
I don't want a game that I can't play;
I don't want a donkey that won't bray;
I don't want a fish pond like Fred's;
I don't want one of those baby sleds;
I don't want paints that are no good;
I don't want building-blocks of wood;
I don't want *you* to think I am queer;
Nor I don't want you to think I don't want anything this year.

> Yours truly,
> JOHNNY.

P.S.—I was just about not to say,
I don't want you to forget me Christmas Day.

Montrose J. Moses

SANTA'S TOYS

Santa Claus was driving his reindeer, his teeming sleigh filled with wonders from every region: dolls that walked and talked and sang, fit for princesses; sleds fine enough for princes, drums and trumpets and swords for young heroes; horses that looked as though they were alive and would spring next moment from their rockers; bats and balls that almost started of themselves from their places; little uniforms, and frocks; skates; tennis-racquets; baby caps and rattles; tiny engines and coaches; railway trains; animals that ran about; steamships; books; pictures—everything to delight the soul of childhood and gratify the affection of age. . . .

from *Santa Claus's Partner* (1899)
by Thomas Nelson Page

THE CHRISTMAS TREE IN THE NURSERY

With wild surprise
Four great eyes
In two small heads
From neighboring beds
Looked out—and winked—
And glittered and blinked
At a very queer sight
In the dim dawn-light.
As plain as can be
A fairy tree
Flashes and glimmers
And shakes and shimmers.
Red, green, and blue
Meet their view;
Silver and gold
Sharp eyes behold;
Small moons, big stars;
And jams in jars,
And cakes and honey,
And thimbles and money,
Pink dogs, blue cats,
Little squeaking rats,
And candles and dolls,
And crackers and polls,
A real bird that sings,
And tokens and favors,
And all sorts of things
For the little shavers.
Four black eyes
Grow big with surprise,
And then grow bigger
When a tiny figure,
Jaunty and airy,
A fairy! a fairy!
From the tree-top cries,
"Open wide! Black Eyes!
Come, children, wake now!
Your joys you may take now!"

Quick as you can think
Twenty small toes
In four pretty rows,
Like little piggies pink,
All kick in the air—
And before you can wink
The tree stands bare!

Richard Watson Gilder

IS THERE A SANTA CLAUS?

. . . Yes, Virginia, there is a Santa Claus. He exists as certainly as love and generosity and devotion exist, and you know that they abound and give to your life its highest beauty and joy. Alas! how dreary would be the world if there were no Santa Claus! It would be as dreary as if there were no Virginias. There would be no childlike faith then, no poetry, no romance to make tolerable this existence. We should have no enjoyment, except in sense and sight. The eternal light with which childhood fills the world would be extinguished.

Not believe in Sant Claus! You might as well not believe in fairies! You might get your papa to hire men to watch in all the chimneys on Christmas Eve to catch Santa Claus, but even if they did not see Santa Claus coming down, what would that prove? Nobody sees Santa Claus, but that is no sign that there is no Santa Claus. The most real things in the world are those that no children or men can see. Did you ever see fairies dancing on the lawn? Of course not, but that's no proof that they are not there. Nobody can conceive or imagine all the wonders there are unseen or unseeable in the world. . . .

No Santa Claus! Thank God he lives, and he lives forever. A thousand years from now, Virginia, nay, ten times ten thousand years from now, he will continue to make glad the heart of childhood.

Francis P. Church's editorial in *The New York Sun*
(September 21, 1897) in response to a letter from
eight-year-old Virginia O'Hanlon

Minor American Holidays, Past and Present

MARTIN LUTHER KING'S BIRTHDAY, *January 15.* He was compared to Gandhi for his methods, accomplishments, and his unshakable faith in nonviolence. He was a gifted orator who breathed vitality and pride into a civil rights movement that shook a nation to its roots and brought millions of blacks closer to enjoying the rights to which they are entitled as citizens and as human beings. Martin Luther King, Jr., winner of the Nobel Peace Prize in 1964, was totally dedicated to a cause. He was a symbol of dignity, strength, and hope to many, and a threatening symbol of unrest and fear to others. From the Birmingham Bus Boycott to his death on a motel balcony in Memphis, he was, by any standard, an important American. The impact of his work is still being felt, and in that he has left a great legacy. The anniversary of his death on April 4, 1968, was commemorated for several years, but gradually his birthday has become the chosen date on which to honor his memory. Although January 15th is not a national holiday, Federal workers are allowed an absence as part of their leave. Some states are now declaring the day a holiday for their civil servants. Schools close for the day in New York City, Philadelphia, Baltimore, Kansas City, and in several other major cities. In some districts where schools remain open, special programs are presented by and for the students. In the private sector, most businesses remain open, but many employers allow the day off as an optional holiday or as personal leave.

ROBERT E. LEE'S BIRTHDAY, *January 19.* To his contemporaries, Robert E. Lee seemed to come from a higher place. His noble bearing and dignity marked him as a man apart, above envy. His deportment on the field of battle bore the stamp of genius. Lee had, as a junior officer on General Winfield Scott's staff during the Mexican War, earned Scott's assessment as "the very best soldier I ever saw in the field." Although he was a scion of Virginia's most distinguished family, Lee learned frugality at an early age. A financial debacle sent his father, "Light Horse Harry" Lee, to debtor's prison when Robert was only two years old. He grew into adulthood as a highly motivated and religious individual. Following his exemplary West Point years, Lee married Mary Anne Randolph Custis, the great-granddaughter of Martha Washington, who bore him seven children. Lee steadily advanced through the ranks, his career assured. The vagaries of history, however, urged a fateful decision on the colonel of the First United States Cavalry. Secessionist fever gripped the South. Seven states broke with the Union in early 1861 and divided the loyalties of the Border States. When Virginia succumbed, Lee followed his conscience. He refused a possible command of an invading Union army and threw in his lot with the state of his birth. When he received his first field command from President Jefferson Davis in mid-1862, a Union army under McClellan had already advanced to within six miles of Richmond. Lee's campaign broke the siege and forced a Federal retreat. The immediate threat to Virginia was eliminated by Lee's masterminding of a major victory at the Second Battle of Bull Run. As the war drew on, General Lee was forced by dwindling resources into an increasingly defensive posture, and the inevitable surrender came at Appomattox in 1865. In peacetime Lee turned to rebuilding. He became president of bankrupt Washington College, now known as Washington and Lee University. Although he was denied American citizenship after the Civil War, Robert E. Lee was an ardent supporter of reconciliation. His greatness was an inspiration and deserves to be remembered. January 19th is a holiday throughout the South.

INAUGURATION DAY, *January 20.* The ascension to the highest elective office in the land is accompanied by much ballyhoo in Washington, D.C., where it is a legal holiday. The spectacle is increased when a new party assumes the reins of power—some say this is in anticipation of sharing the spoils. Inauguration Day is a media day, too. Networks flash to the preparatory details during TV news broadcasts and offer full coverage of the event itself. The new president and vice president of the United States are sworn in by the chief justice of the Supreme Court under the gaze of millions. Mere thousands witnessed earlier inaugurations, the first three of which were not in Washington. George Washington took his first oath of office on the steps of City Hall when New York City was the capital, and in front of Independence Hall when Philadelphia was the seat of power. Nor did the date remain constant. George Washington's first inauguration was on April 30, 1789, but other inaugurations were held on March 4th, a date that was changed by the Twentieth Amendment in 1933 to its present celebration on January 20th. As the ceremonies became more of a public event, more room was needed to accommodate the crowds. When Andrew Jackson became president, supporters came by the thousands from the West and South. Following James Monroe's lead, the oath was administered on the eastern portico of the Capitol to the approval of the throngs. It is still the favored spot from which to deliver the inaugural address. After the formalities, a large parade is formed which includes marching bands and soldiers. The day ends with a gala formal ball. Probably no other world leader, excluding monarchs and self-proclaimed emperors, is ushered to the pinnacle of power amid such pomp and circumstance.

NATIONAL FREEDOM DAY, *February 1.* In Abraham Lincoln's own estimation, the Emancipation Proclamation was "the central act of my Administration and the greatest event of the nineteenth century." It was not law, however. It would take from the Preliminary Proclamation of September 22, 1862, to December 18, 1865, for the policy to become a ratified Constitutional Amendment affecting the whole nation. Initially, the Proclamation applied only to the South. Millions hailed the event: finally, Negro slaves were to be unshackled in every sense of the word. As the furious military compaigns raged in the South, abolitionists redoubled their efforts in the states and in Congress. The Republican Party nominated Lincoln for a second term and pledged in its platform to end slavery. Meanwhile, Maryland, Missouri, and Louisiana abolished slavery on their own. In early 1865, after considerable debate, both the House and Senate approved a resolution that would allow an amendment to circulate among the states for ratification. By the end of December, slavery was abolished forever. The actual Emancipation Day, January 1, was unofficially celebrated for years. In some places, the date of the arrival of Union troops was commemorated. National Freedom Day was not observed as a national occasion until President Harry S. Truman signed a proclamation in 1948. February 1st was chosen because it was the day Lincoln signed the congressional resolution to give it added weight before going to the states for ratification. The official abolition of slavery in the United States was a milestone in the struggle to fulfill the ideals and promise of the Constitution. The Thirteenth Amendment was a first step toward the realization of a dream.

GROUND-HOG DAY, *February 2.* With Christmas behind us and a blustery January under our belts, we begin to tire of treacherous footing and frost-nipped fingers. It is almost in desperation that on February 2nd we can pretend to be a ground hog if the forecast suits our mood. Perversely, we wish for clouds, for, if it's clear, "there'll be two winters in the year." Unlike the ground hog, however, we cannot hibernate. We must take what nature serves us. If we are lucky enough not to cast a shadow, we are elevated by the illusion that warmth and vitality will soon be upon us. If there is a shadow at our feet, we must brush aside a momentary shade of gloom and push on, denying in our urbane way that such a primitive, folksy prognosticator could have any use at all. Ground-Hog Day is the American version of Candlemas Day. It came by way of Germany, England, and Scotland, where it has been the subject of popular rhymes. Although Candlemas is a religious observance, there is no apparent relationship between the purification of the Virgin Mary and folk meteorology. The Slumbering Ground Hog Lodge in Lancaster County, Pennsylvania, fancies itself as the more-or-less official interpreter of the grizzly marmot's emergence. If he sees his shadow, six more weeks of winter are assured. If it's cloudy and he doesn't see any shadow, he will not return to his burrow to continue his sleep because an early spring is at hand.

If Candlemas Day be fair and bright,
Winter will have another flight;
But if it be dark with clouds and rain,
Winter is gone, and will not come again.

ALAMO DAY, *March 6.* The stand of a handful of men in an old San Antonio mission lends itself well to characterization in sweeping, historic terms. The significance of the event as a symbol of resistance to authoritarian dictatorship was well recognized, even as it was happening. The Mexican General Santa Anna and 2,400 troops lay siege to the temporary fortress from February 23, 1836, to March 6, finally killing all its 182 defenders. American settlers had been colonizing the Mexican-owned Texas since 1821, when Stephen Austin established the first colony. Mexico had only recently achieved its own independence and was hoping to establish democratic institutions. Instability led to the rise to power of Santa Anna, who quickly proved unfaithful to the new constitution. Texans did not mix well with Mexican authority. They were especially incensed by the ban on any religious observances but those of the Roman Catholic Church. It also seemed that the government was too remote to respond to their needs as citizens. Texans were poorly represented in Saltillo, the capital. Concerned that the colonists might get out of hand, Santa Anna sent a cavalry detachment to Gonzalez. Fighting erupted when the town refused to hand over its cannon. The troop was put to flight. Texans knew that an army would return in time. A small force of Americans took San Antonio and occupied the most defensible position, the Alamo. Among the brave but doomed contingent were Jim Bowie, Davy Crockett, and Colonel William B. Travis. When the attack came, they knew defeat was inevitable. Their bravery became martyrdom and inspired Sam Houston's army to victory six weeks later at San Jacinto. More importantly, the defense of the

Alamo delayed Santa Anna for two weeks, long enough for General Houston to assemble and prepare his men for battle. Texans are justly proud of their heritage. Their spirit of independence is part of a great American tradition.

PAN AMERICAN DAY, *April 14.* To most of us, an American is a citizen of the United States. For the celebrants of Pan American Day, the word has a larger meaning. Residents of the New World are Americans all, and this holiday exists to foster intercontinental solidarity and cooperation. The event is proclaimed annually in this country by the President of the United States and is observed by members of the Organization of American States. It commemorates the day in 1890 when a resolution of the first International Conference of American States established the International Bureau of American Republics, later called the Pan American Union and finally the Organization of American States (OAS). The date was not formally noted until 1931 when President Herbert Hoover declared April 14th Pan American Day. Although the day passes with few Americans aware of its existence, diplomats in North and South America mark the occasion with dinners and other formal gatherings. Libraries often assemble special displays to highlight the literature and culture of the Americas while schools may devote the day to lessons or pageants with an international flavor. The OAS takes this annual opportunity to promote in the most public way the spirit of unity and exchange which it works toward all year round. One of the reasons that Pan American Day falls on April 14th is that in nearly all the American republics, school is in session at that time.

PATRIOTS' DAY, *Third Monday in April.* Running an empire is such an expensive proposition! The thirteen American Colonies were a marvelous source for natural resources and taxes. Unfortunately for Mother England, her needs were not the needs of an increasingly independent and therefore annoying string of Colonies. Merchants in such northern port cities as Boston were especially noisome. They just couldn't buy the British argument that higher revenues were needed to defray the costs of maintaining garrisons on the frontier to keep the Indians at bay. The measures imposed by King George III's government seemed restrictive, cavalier, and ultimately punitive. Not all Colonists suffered equally. Some even profited. But enough were incensed that bonds of rebellious cooperation began to draw the Colonies together. The Townshend Acts stirred such ire among Bostonians that a band of men stole aboard three ships in Boston Harbor and dumped the cargoes of tea into the water. News of the Boston Tea Party spread. Britain responded with further restrictions while Colonists organized and became more intransigent. Military preparations were undertaken. In Massachusetts, the Provincial Congress purged the militia of Loyalists. Concord, a small community near Boston, became a major storage point for munitions and weapons. Upon learning of the cache, the British dispatched 700 men to seize and destroy it. Patriots got word of the secret expedition in advance, and messengers were sent to forewarn sympathizers. Despite the capture of Paul Revere, seventy men were roused from bed and assembled on the green at Lexington, two-thirds of the way to Concord. A brief skirmish ensued when the Patriots stood their ground, leaving eight dead. The British proceeded to Concord where they destroyed the stores that hadn't already been hidden. Meanwhile 400 armed Patriots gathered across the Concord River and engaged the bridge guard before the British repulsed them. Their task successfully done, the Redcoats began to march back to Boston. Angry rebels harried and ambushed them all along the way. By the end of the day, nearly 300 British soldiers lay dead. The Revolution was afoot. April 19, 1775, was a historic day, indeed.

LOYALTY DAY, *May 1.* Loyalty Day doesn't spring from the memory of a particular event in American history. Rather, it came into being as a reaction to May Day celebrations in the Soviet Union. May Day was designated "Labor Day" by Socialists in 1889 and became a major holiday after the Revolution brought Lenin to power in 1917. By the 1930s, the Communists were attracting world-wide attention with their massive parades of military might. Disturbed by what seemed to be a growing threat to democratic principles, the Veterans of Foreign Wars began to sponsor events on May 1st designed to ignite similar patriotic demonstrations in the United States. They worked hard to promote what they called Loyalty Day. Schools, labor unions, churches, and other patriotic groups were encouraged to sponsor plays, essay contests, and special programs with patriotic themes. Following World War II and its enforced cooperation of East and West, forty-nine state and territorial governors proclaimed Loyalty Day. Through the 1950s, interest persisted in declaring a national day, which finally achieved Congressional approval in 1958. Typically, Loyalty Day observers invoke such things as the bravery of early patriots who fought and died for the cause of freedom, the stirring words of famous statesmen and poets, and historic events that have shaped our destiny. They call on fellow Americans to consider their great heritage and rededicate themselves to the ideals of the Founding Fathers, that these ideals may be preserved in a threatened world. Loyalty Day observances have flagged in recent years, but the feeling of pride in America remains strong in the hearts of most citizens.

CINCO DE MAYO, *May 5.* From the Spanish conquest of the Aztecs in 1521 to the revolutionary period in the 20th century, Mexico was in almost constant turmoil. Her wealth in precious metals brought soldiers and businessmen in search of wealth and power. Avarice flourished under the tropical sun, bringing suffering first to the Indians, and later to generations of mixed blood. Periods of great reform were followed by years of dictatorial rule. Mexico has always been the stage for mighty struggles. The holiday of Cinco de Mayo commemorates the efforts of Mexicans to retain their national independence. It is still a historic day and is celebrated by Mexican-Americans in the southwestern United States. In 1855, a massive reform movement set about redistributing the wealth of large landholders and the Church. After much bloodletting, the liberal regime took the reigns of power. Benito Juarez, an Indian and a hero of the people, became president of a paralyzed nation. The banished conservatives sought the aid of France's Emperor Napoleon III, who saw the opportunity to enlarge his empire. Mexico's inability to pay international debts gave Napoleon the pretext for military intervention. In 1862, a French army set out to conquer Mexico City on the same route Cortes had taken. The Mexican army fell back in advance of the 6,000 seasoned troops. They decided to make their stand at Puebla, halfway to the capital. Poorly trained and underequipped, the defenders met the French attack on the 5th of May. After four hours, and with the help of heavy rains, the Mexicans routed the would-be French conquerors.

The battle was an inspiration, but in the end, the French prevailed. They sent 30,000 troops to take the capital, only to abandon Mexico in 1867.

ARMED FORCES DAY, *Third Saturday in May.* The Army, Navy, and Air Force throw open their doors once a year on Armed Forces Day. Americans get the chance to witness our armed might in public displays of weaponry on the land and sea and in the air. At some facilities, the officers' club golf course becomes the scene of a mock infantry battle for the benefit of a wide-eyed gallery of visitors. Overseas bases are also opened up to the nationals of their host countries. It is a day when flags fly and banners proclaim the theme of "Power for Peace." The First Armed Forces Day was proclaimed by President Harry S. Truman in 1950. It is established anew each year, but is not considered a legal or public holiday. The event serves to remind all of us of the debt we owe to our fighting men and women. Their sacrifices have been mighty. The proud history of our armed forces reaches back to 1775, the year of the establishment of the Army, Navy, and Marines. Each banch, including the Air Force, has distinguished itself for its fighting spirit in wartime and its readiness in time of peace. Armed Forces Day does not mark a specific anniversary. Each of the Services has its own day to commemorate its birth. Army Day is April 6th, Navy Day is October 27th, and Air Force Day falls on the second Saturday in September. These are not considered public occasions. Such recognition is reserved for Armed Forces Day.

JEFFERSON DAVIS'S BIRTHDAY, *June 3.* Early in his life, Jeferson Davis seemed marked for success. A graduate of West Point, he distinguished himself in the Black Hawk and Mexican wars. As a wealthy plantation owner, he was assured of at least a local sphere of influence. But through a fortunate marriage and a politically-inclined older brother, he became interested in a larger realm of politics in Mississippi. In the U.S. Senate he became the leading spokesman for the South upon the death of John Calhoun. An ardent expansionist who argued against the compromise that allowed California to enter the Union as a free state, Davis resigned his seat but was unable to resist the lure of national politics. By the time he was chosen President of the Confederacy, Davis had, ironically, mellowed in his fervor for secession. He counseled moderation and hoped to avert bloodshed. The capture of Fort Sumter by a Southern army unleashed a military fury beyond the control of any man. Like General Robert E. Lee, Davis had to make do with ever-dwindling resources. Conscription replaced dependence on Southern volunteers. Southern railroads couldn't keep the armies supplied. A Northern blockade tightened constantly. Foreign states failed to recognize Southern legitimacy. When Richmond finally fell in 1865, Davis fled and was captured. He spent two years in prison. During his declining years in Mississippi, he tried to pick up the pieces with ill-fated business ventures. He died in 1889. Jefferson Davis's birthday is a legal holiday in nearly every Southern state. Some states celebrate both the birthday and a Confederate Memorial Day. Each is the occasion for dinners and graveside ceremonies honoring the war dead.

BUNKER HILL DAY, *June 17.* If there was any doubt about the seriousness of the American Patriots' intention to throw off the British yoke, it was dispelled by the Battle of Bunker Hill on June 17, 1775. American troop strength had risen to 16,000 around Boston. They surrounded 10,000 of His Majesty's forces under the command of General Gage. His back to the water, Gage declared martial law in Boston on June 12th. He offered amnesty to all but Samuel Adams and John Hancock in return for allegiance to the Crown. An armed engagement was assured when it became known that Gage was going to move on Bunker Hill and Dorchester Heights. The American Colonel Prescott was ordered to take and fortify the hill before Gage could march. On the night of the 16th, Prescott went beyond Bunker Hill to Breed's Hill which overlooked the harbor. Hurriedly, his men erected fortifications. At daybreak, surprised at what they saw above them, the British artillery and naval cannon opened up. Under fire, Prescott's men continued to improve their redoubt. By late morning, fortifications were being thrown up on Bunker Hill. The British moved steadily, but at considerable expense, toward the rebel position. Two attacks were repulsed. Finally, when the Patriots' ammunition was exhausted, a bayonet charge carried the hill. The British lost over 1,000 men, while the Americans lost 450. The battle was an American loss in the sense that the British had accomplished their objective. It was, however, an inspriation to Patriots throughout the Colonies. It also served notice to the British government that subduing its naughty Colonies would require a great expenditure of resources because the Americans would resist them and fight them every step of the way. Today, celebrations of Bunker Hill Day are limited to the Boston area.

CITIZENSHIP DAY, *September 17.* Despite the periodic effort of powerful interests to influence the massive flow of immigrants to the United States, millions of diverse peoples have become citizens and have contributed to our greatness as a nation. During each new wave of immigration, millions had to confront the obstacles of language, custom, poverty, and finding a place to call home. Many of these newcomers had to face the additional barriers of color, race, and religion. During the early 19th century, traditional Anglo-American ideals were thought to be threatened by an influx of Germans and Roman-Catholic Irish. Nativists became a significant political force in some areas and agitated to raise the residency requirement to twenty-one years before citizenship—and therefore the right to vote—could be granted. Their dire predictions never came true, of course, and in time the Irish and Northern Europeans gained respectability and became an integral part of the social fabric. They were replaced as objects of scorn by the specter of Mediterranean and Eastern European immigrants who, in their turn, have achieved a great measure of success in the twentieth century. Racist legislation in the 1880s and early 1900s forbade the passage of Asians to American shores. The ban was not lifted until 1952, the year Citizenship Day was born. It combines the spirit of Constitution Day with that of I Am An American Day, holidays which it replaced. Traditionally, Citizenship Day has included swearing-in ceremonies for new citizens. Activities are sometimes slated for a whole week and might include patriotic displays, voter registration drives, and re-enactments of the signing of the Constitution, which took place in Philadelphia on September 17, 1787.

AMERICAN INDIAN DAY, *Usually the fourth Friday in September.* The first American Indian Day was celebrated in Rochester, New York, in 1912. Dr. Arthur C. Parker of the Rochester Museum of Arts and Sciences was the moving force behind the festivities. For three years the Boy Scouts observed the day with activities devoted to Indian lore, crafts, and customs. An effort to honor native Americans on a national level was initiated in 1914, when Red Fox James, a Montana Blackfoot, covered 4,000 miles between state capitals on horseback in an attempt to solicit support. His journey culminated in a visit to the White House and the delivery of an appeal signed by twenty-four governors. This equestrian odyssey did not bring about a national day, however, but several states do observe the fourth Friday in September. Some other states in which the day is noted change it from year to year. The American Indian is the true native American. Anthropologists have unearthed evidence of Indian habitation that precedes the birth of Christ by 4,000 years. During the scant few centuries following the Age of Discovery, the Indian became an alien in his own land, dispossessed, uprooted, decimated by numerically and technologically superior Europeans. Between 1492 and 1900, the Indian population dropped from an estimated 1.1 million to 250,000. The European approach to life was questing, objective, and exploitative. It left no room for appreciation of a world view according to which the Indian lived in a fundamental unity with nature. He responded to the changing of the seasons, and accepted, contributed to, and transmitted a rich and varied cultural heritage. It is not surprising, given this cultural and philosophical chasm which separated Indians and new settlers, that for centuries Indians were viewed as shiftless and indolent. Today, a worldwide trend toward ethnic pride and national solidarity has given American Indians renewed hope that their own ancient traditions will perpetuate. Legal battles have in some cases restored ancestral homelands. The "back to nature" movement of the '60s and '70s has greatly contributed to interest in Indian culture and customs among non-Indians. American Indian Day honors these traditions.

LEIF ERICSON DAY, *October 9.* Historians tell us that, in all likelihood, Leif Ericson visited the shores of North America 500 years before Columbus sailed into the West Indies. The small Viking settlements on the coast of Greenland were closer to what is now Labrador than to their Scandinavian homelands. Leif Ericson's hot-tempered grandfather, Thorvald, was banished from Norway for murder. He settled in Iceland, where his son, Eric the Red, committed the same act with the same result. He fled further westward, to an island he dubbed Greenland. Leif was a more temperate man, filled with vigor and curiosity. He returned to Norway laden with furs for King Olaf Tryggvesson. During his stay at the royal court he became a Christian. The story is told that during the voyage back to Greenland, Leif's small ships were blown off course by a terrific storm. After forty days at sea, the thankful seamen landed on the coast of North America. The scholarly interpretation attributed this first discovery to another sailor under similar circumstances while Leif Ericson was in Norway. Leif supposedly heard of the story and was filled with curiosity. Setting out to see for himself, he probably made landfalls in Labrador, Newfoundland, and finally at Cape Cod or Long Island, the latter of which he called Vineland the Good. His discoveries seem not to have stirred the imaginations of his countrymen, for no major colonization efforts followed. However, evidence of one settlement in Newfoundland has been dated by archeologists at about 1000 A.D., shortly after Ericson's journey. The voyage of Christopher Columbus in 1492 had greater historical impact because, unlike Ericson's discovery, it was not almost immediately forgotten. It came at a time when the European world was receptive to the results of far-flung expeditions. In fact, the spirit of the time demanded exploration.

UNITED NATIONS DAY, *October 24.* It was Woodrow Wilson's dream to see a peaceful world governed by enlightened men whose differences could be resolved rationally in an international forum. The League of Nations was the expression of that dream, a response to the horrors of a World War. The United Nations, too, was founded after a great war, even more awesome than the first. It combines the idealism inherent in the hope for global peace with the lessons learned from the failure of the League. On October 24, 1945, a majority of member states ratified the United Nations Charter. Each year these nations and dozens of newer members reflect on the aims and achievements of the United Nations. Its role as peacemaker has involved it in nearly all the world's hot-spots since its inception. Soldiers of many nations have stood between warring factions while diplomats have tried to reach accord. U.N. intervention in the Middle East may yet prove indispensable to the cause of peace. Just as dramatic, if less publicized, are the organization's efforts to combat hunger and disease. Thousands upon thousands can thank the U.N. for disaster relief and medical assistance. UNICEF and the World Health Organization are two agencies that are engaged in a constant struggle to care for those who are least able to care for themselves. The U.N. also provides extensive technical assistance and supports a wide range of research projects aimed at fostering social and economic growth in underdeveloped areas. United Nations Day is an opportunity to highlight not only the work of the organization, but the ideals which gave it birth. Schools and libraries offer units, displays, and assemblies with international themes. Millions of children and adults are reminded at least once a year that, in these times of precarious peace, there is still hope.

ELECTION DAY, *First Tuesday after the first Monday in November.* The simple matter of casting a ballot is something many of us take for granted. In fact, many citizens don't even bother to vote, especially in local elections, where their ballot counts the most. Americans are fortunate that, with few exceptions in recent years, elections are run honestly. In many countries, election day is a sham, more of a public relations gimmick than a measure of the will of the people. Today, the right to vote is granted to all American citizens over the age of eighteen. It was not always so easy. Early in our history only landowners and those belonging to certain churches were permitted to vote. And of course, these could only be men. In some places educational requirements were added. As women became more educated throughout the nineteenth century, they brought great pressure to bear on the opponents of universal suffrage. It was not until 1920, however, that the Nineteenth Amendment granted the long-fought-for right to vote. Similar struggles have been waged by other disenfranchised groups, such as Indians and Negroes. After the Civil War, in the chaos of Restoration, many blacks were elected to public office in the South. When the Southern white power structure recovered sufficiently to wield political clout, blacks were effectively prevented from voting by measures like the Jim Crow laws. It was not until the 1960s that the civil rights movement was able to make headway against generations of exclusionary practices. Voter registration drives have made the "black vote" an important consideration in American politics. A specific Election Day was not chosen until 1845, when the present arrangement became law. Presidential elections are held every four years. Senators are chosen every six years. Members of the House of Representatives come up for election every other year.

BILL OF RIGHTS DAY, *December 15.* America's first national government was the Articles of Confederation. It was forged in the vacuum left by British defeat at the hands of the Colonists. The authors, wearied by decades of arbitrary centralized government, reacted by forming a loose confederacy of states. It soon became clear that such a system was unworkable. A stronger central government was essential. As a result, our present Constitution, controversial to be sure, was forged in 1787. Richard Henry Lee summed up the difficulty with the document: "Where is the contract between the nation and the government? The Constitution makes no mention but of those who govern, and never speaks of the rights of the people who are governed." A reasonable solution was worked out by 1791 with the addition of ten amendments, which became known as the Bill of Rights. Among these guaranteed rights are freedom of religion, of the press, of free speech; and the right to peaceful assembly; the right to bear arms; the right to due process of law, trial by jury, and freedom from cruel and unusual punishment. Many additional amendments have been added since then, but the orignal ten have stood the test of time. We take them for granted today, but it is only because of the sensitivity and foresight of the Founding Fathers that such a document exists. The first Bill of Rights Day was proclaimed by President Franklin D. Roosevelt on December 15, 1941, 150 years after it became part of the Constitution and eight days after the surprise attack on Pearl Harbor. It was a dramatic occasion to reaffirm our national purpose in the face of the grim threat posed by the totalitarian regimes of Hitler in Europe and the Japanese Empire in the Pacific. We continue to mark the day by displaying flags and witnessing activities sponsored by patriotic and civic groups.

FOREFATHERS' DAY, *December 21.* Perhaps the generations that followed the landing of the Pilgrims at Plymouth Rock were too busy with the business of carving out a living to celebrate the historic arrival of their forefathers on December 21, 1620. Nearly 150 years elapsed before the hearty young members of the Old Colony Club convened to feast in a fashion appropriate to the austere circumstances of 1620. The story of Plymouth Rock might never have survived the eighteenth century were it not for Ephraim Spooner, who at the age of six was present at the final visit to the Rock, in 1741, of Ruling Elder Thomas Faunce. The 95-year-old Faunce, the son of a Pilgrim family, had heard that a wharf was to be built over the Rock. He wanted one last glimpse of the site upon which his family had landed. Spooner kept the memory alive, and when he and some other well-to-do men of the Plymouth area decided to form a social club in 1769, they dedicated their association to the founders of the Old Colony and celebrated the date of their arrival at the site visited by Elder Faunce. Festivities were repeated in each of the next three years, but, with the air of rebellion thickening after the Boston Tea Party, the Club divided against itself and disbanded. Public celebrations followed, including one in 1774, during which the local Sons of Liberty decided to move the Rock. It split in two under the strain of thirty oxen teams, but the Patriots were undeterred. They dragged the top half to the Town Square where it remained for sixty years. Subsequent Forefathers' Days were neither especially noteworthy nor regular until the bicentennial of 1820, when Daniel Webster orated upon the Day for two hours. The tercentennial was celebrated 101 years later. It was delayed because the sea, receding over the years, had left the Rock dry and threatened to destroy the credibility of the landing story. Town fathers, fearing a loss of tourist trade, had the Rock moved to the tidewater under a hastily erected canopy. The Rock failed to cooperate—it broke up, causing a postponement of the event. Forefather's Day is a regional celebration today, but is noted by New England Societies across the United States.

Selected Bibliography

Achelis, Elisabeth. *Of Time and the Calendar.* New York: Hermitage House, 1955.

Barnett, James H. *The American Christmas.* New York: The Macmillan Co., 1954.

Baur, John E. *Christmas on the American Frontier, 1800–1900.* Caldwell, Idaho: The Caxton Printers, 1961.

Botkin, B. A., ed. *A Treasury of American Folklore.* New York: Crown Publishers, 1944.

Buck, A. M. *My Saint Patrick.* Boston: Lothrop, Lee and Shepherd, 1937.

Carruth, Gorton, and Associates. *Encyclopedia of American Facts and Dates.* New York: Thomas Y. Crowell, 1965.

Chambers, Robert. *Book of Days: A Miscellany of Popular Antiquities.* 2 vols. Philadelphia: J. B. Lippincott Co., n.d. [Originally published by W. & R. Chambers, London and Edinburgh, 1864.]

Count, Earl W. *Four Thousand Years of Christmas.* New York: Henry Schuman, 1948.

Craven, Wesley Frank. *The Legend of the Founding Fathers.* New York: New York University Press, 1956.

Deems, Edward M. *Holy Days and Holidays.* New York: Funk & Wagnalls Co., 1902.

Ditchfield, P. H., *Old English Customs.* New York: New Amsterdam Book Company, 1896.

Dorson, Richard M. *American Folklore.* Chicago: University of Chicago Press, 1959.

Douglas, George William. Rev. by Helen Douglas Compton. *The American Book of Days.* New York: The H. W. Wilson Co., 1937, 1948.

Dunphy, Hubert M. *Christmas Every Christmas.* Milwaukee: The Bruce Publishing Co., 1960.

Dupuy, Trevor Nevitt, ed. *Holidays: Days of Significance for All Americans.* New York: Franklin Watts, 1965.

Fern, Vergilius. *A Brief Dictionary of American Superstitions.* New York: Philosophical Library, 1965.

Forster, T. *The Perennial Calendar and Companion to the Almanack.* London: Harding, Mavor and Lepard, 1824.

Greif, Martin. *The St. Nicholas Book: A Celebration of Christmas Past.* New York: Universe Books, 1976.

Harper, Howard V. *Days and Customs of All Faiths.* New York: Fleet Publishing Corp., 1957.

Hazeltine, Mary Emogene. *Anniversaries and Holidays.* Chicago: American Library Association, 1928.

Hazlitt, William Carew. *Dictionary of Faiths and Folklore.* London: Reeves and Turner, 1905.

Hutchison, Ruth, and Ruth Adams. *Every Day's a Holiday.* New York: Harper & Brothers, 1951.

James, E. O. *Seasonal Feasts and Festivals.* New York: Barnes & Noble, 1961.

Kane, Joseph Nathan. *Famous First Facts.* New York: The H. W. Wilson Co., 1933.

Keller, Helen Rex. *Dictionary of Dates.* 2 vols. New York: The Macmillan Co., 1934.

Krythe, Maymie. *All About American Holidays.* New York: Harper & Row, 1962.

Lang, Andrew. *Custom and Myth.* New York: Harper & Brothers, 1885.

Linton, Ralph and Adelin. *We Gather Together.* New York: Henry Schuman, 1949.

———. *Halloween Through Twenty Centuries.* New York: Henry Schuman, 1950.

Lord, Priscilla Sawyer and Daniel J. Foley. *Easter Garland.* Philadelphia: Chilton Books, 1963.

McSpadden, J. Walker. *The Book of Holidays.* New York: Thomas Y. Crowell, 1917.

Myers, Robert J. with the Editors of Hallmark Cards. *Celebrations: The Complete Book of American Holidays.* Garden City, New York: Doubleday & Company, Inc., 1972. [Indispensable for the modern reader.]

Quaife, Milo M., Melvin J. Weig, and Roy E. Appleman. *The History of the United States Flag.* New York: Harper & Row, 1961.

Radford, E. and M. A. M., eds. Rev. by Christina Hole. *Encyclopedia of Superstitions.* London: Hutchinson & Co., 1961.

Rice, Susan Tracy, comp., and Robert Haven Schauffler, ed. *Mother's Day.* New York: Dodd, Mead & Co., 1915.

Schauffler, Robert Haven. *Arbor Day.* New York: Moffat, Yard & Co., 1909.

———. *Thanksgiving.* New York: Moffat, Yard & Co., 1907.

———. *Washington's Birthday.* New York: Moffat, Yard & Co., 1916.

Scherer, Margaret R. *Thanksgiving and Harvest Festivals.* New York: The Metropolitan Museum of Art, 1942.

Smith, Bradley. *Columbus in the New World.* Garden City, New York: Doubleday & Co., 1962.

Spicer, Dorothy Gladys. *Yearbook of English Festivals.* New York: The H. W. Wilson Co., 1954.

Tittle, Walter, comp. *Colonial Holidays.* Garden City, New York: Doubleday, Page & Co., 1910.

Vipont, Elfrida. *Some Christian Festivals.* London: Michael Joseph, Ltd., 1963.

Walsh, William S. *Curiosities of Popular Customs.* Philadelphia: J. B. Lippincott Co., 1898.

Watts, Alan. *Easter: Its Story and Meaning.* New York: Henry Schuman, 1950.

Weiser, Francis X. *The Holyday Book.* New York: Harcourt, Brace & Co., 1956.

———. *The Christmas Book.* New York: Harcourt, Brace & Co., 1952.

Whitney, David C. *Founders of Freedom in America: Lives of the Men Who Signed the Declaration of Independence.* Chicago: J. G. Ferguson Publishing Co., 1964.